Engagement with North Korea

A Portfolio-Based Approach to Diplomacy

RAFIQ DOSSANI

Prepared for the Korea Foundation

RAND NATIONAL SECURITY RESEARCH DIVISION

For more information on this publication, visit www.rand.org/t/RRA432-1

Library of Congress Cataloging-in-Publication Data is available for this publication.
ISBN: 978-1-9774-0600-2

Published by the RAND Corporation, Santa Monica, Calif.

Cover illustration: Wildpixel/iStockphoto.

Preface

Following the failure of recent efforts by the United States to engage North Korea in denuclearization talks, we proposed and tested an approach to negotiations that addresses the reasons for past failures. The purpose of this study is methodological: to propose and test a novel approach to negotiations, termed the *portfolio method*. The elements of the portfolio method are (1) the inclusion of countries with national interests that overlap those of the United States and North Korea, (2) prior agreement on the goals of negotiation between the negotiating parties, (3) the inclusion of primarily hard commitments in agreements, (4) the incorporation of the preferences of in-country stakeholders, (5) the linking of multiple areas of negotiation, and (6) trust-building mechanisms.

This research was sponsored by the Korea Foundation and conducted within the International Security and Defense Policy Center of the RAND National Security Research Division (NSRD). NSRD conducts research and analysis for the Office of the Secretary of Defense, the U.S. Intelligence Community, U.S. State Department, allied foreign governments, and foundations.

For more information on the RAND International Security and Defense Policy Center, see www.rand.org/nsrd/isdp or contact the Center director (contact information is provided on the webpage).

Contents

Preface ... iii
Figure and Boxes ... vii
Tables ... ix
Summary ... xi
Acknowledgments ... xv
Abbreviations ... xvii

CHAPTER ONE
Introduction ... 1
Step One: Develop the Portfolio Method ... 2
Step Two: Develop Test Cases ... 3
Step Three: Validate Through Expert Dialogue ... 4

CHAPTER TWO
Approach ... 7
Disagreements on the Goals of Negotiations ... 7
Inadequate Domestic and International Support ... 9
Failure to Build Trust ... 14
Discussion of the Logic Model ... 16

CHAPTER THREE
Application of the Logic Model ... 21
Country Selection ... 21
In-Country Stakeholders ... 24
Getting to Agreed Negotiation Goals ... 26
Selecting Action Plans ... 31

Mapping Action Plans to Goals 45
Recommended Action Plans and Portfolios 46
Building Consensus Among In-Country Stakeholders 48

CHAPTER FOUR
Conclusion 55

APPENDIXES
A. Screening of Action Plans 57
B. Measuring Consensus Among In-Country Stakeholders 61
C. Glossary 63

References 65

Figure and Boxes

Figure

2.1. Logic Model 16

Boxes

3.1. List of In-Country Stakeholders, by Country 27
3.2. Proposed Portfolios 52

Tables

2.1. Comparison of Goals and Areas of Negotiation in Past Negotiations and the Portfolio Method 10
2.2. Comparison of Areas of Agreement and Joint Declarations in Past Negotiations and the Portfolio Method 11
2.3. Comparison of Achievements of Past Negotiations 13
2.4. Comparison of the Reasons for Failure of Past Negotiations 15
3.1. Long-Term Goals Regarding North Korea 28
3.2. Summary of DPRK Economic Sanctions 40
3.3. North Korea's Leading Exports 41
3.4. North Korea's Leading Imports 42
3.5. Mapping Action Plans to Goals for the DPRK 46
3.6. Expert-Ranked Action Plans 47
3.7. In-Country Support for Action Plans 50
3.8. Expert-Ranked Action Plans After Consensus Tests 51
3.9. Roles of Stakeholder Countries 53
A.1. CRIVR Screening of Action Plans 58

Summary

In 1994, faced with the threat of North Korea's intent to withdraw from the nuclear Non-Proliferation Treaty, the United States negotiated its first agreement with North Korea. Under the so-called Agreed Framework, North Korea said it would halt its nuclear weapons program in exchange for energy supplies and other assistance. That agreement ultimately collapsed over the next eight years. Twenty-six years and several unsuccessful official dialogues later, the two countries again face rising tension.

In the midst of this impasse in nuclear negotiations with North Korea, we conducted this study to explore whether opportunities for conflict resolution and consensus-building between North Korea and the United States still exist in the current political atmosphere. The challenge is to develop action plans that will successfully engage all sides.

Following the failure of recent efforts by the United States to engage North Korea in denuclearization negotiations, we proposed and tested an approach to negotiations that addresses the reasons for past failures. The purpose of this study is methodological: to explore a novel approach to negotiations, termed the *portfolio method*.

The elements of the portfolio method are (1) the inclusion of countries with national interests that overlap those of the United States and North Korea, (2) prior agreement on the goals of negotiation between the negotiating parties, (3) the inclusion of primarily hard commitments in agreements, (4) the incorporation of the preferences of in-country stakeholders, (5) the linking of multiple areas of negotiation, and (6) trust-building mechanisms.

Although some of these elements were present in earlier negotiations, the portfolio method improves the likelihood of success because it brings together a sufficient number of elements to comprehensively address the reasons for past failure.

To test the portfolio method, we assembled a team of experts, who went through the steps for portfolio creation with actual cases using the portfolio method and provided a review. We used the method of Track II dialogue to assemble experts who are nonstate actors with differing national interests to investigate how breakdowns in negotiations can be addressed.

Thus, this project consists of the following parts: (1) develop the portfolio method, (2) apply it to develop test cases, and (3) validate the test cases using experts.

The expert dialogue proceeded as follows. The action plans were first reviewed for the support they would receive from in-country stakeholders. Only those action plans that passed threshold levels of consensus were considered for final portfolios. Second, experts discussed combinations of action plans that would meet the negotiation goals. Using this discussion, experts proposed three portfolios with different levels of risk, trade-offs, and ongoing commitments. Third, the expert panel identified the roles that stakeholder countries could play with regard to ensuring that the agreements succeed.

The expert dialogue revealed the following:

- The advantages of the portfolio method were (1) prior agreement on the goals of the negotiation, (2) a phased action-for-action set of implementation plans, (3) the inclusion of primarily hard commitments, (4) the incorporation of the preferences of in-country stakeholders, (5) the inclusion and linking of multiple areas of negotiation, and (6) the inclusion of trust-building mechanisms. The disadvantages were (1) the outcomes of the portfolio method were as subject to stress from unexpected external events as other methods and (2) the synergistic value of portfolios—i.e., that the combined portfolio may be better for both sides than the sum of the individual issues, since there may be important interrelationships between the portfolio constituents—did not emerge.

- Experts uniformly welcomed the shift in their typical role from providing analysis, assessment, and recommendations to reviewing RAND Corporation–developed analysis and assessments and developing recommendations because the process provided more depth to the dialogue. However, the proposed action plans lacked the detail that is usually part of actual negotiations. For example, proposals on sanctions relief typically contain such details as the dollar value of reliefs. By contrast, the proposals in our research do not offer such a level of detail. However, experts accepted that the objective of the project was to demonstrate an approach rather than to present detailed action plans. They also noted that dialogues between Track II experts typically tended to also lack such detail.

In summary, we propose in this report an approach (the portfolio method) that explicitly addresses the reasons for past failures. We tested the portfolio method through expert dialogue. We found that the portfolio approach offers promising ways forward for negotiations between North Korea and the United States.

Acknowledgments

This report has benefited from comments by Sohaela Amiri, Naoko Aoki, Bruce Bennett, Hyeon Seon Choi, Jinwoo Lee, and Michael Mazarr. I also acknowledge the helpful comments of the reviewers. I also acknowledge the helpful comments of the reviewers. I am grateful to the panel of experts for their participation in this study.

Abbreviations

CRIVR	contributes, reciprocity, implementable, verifiability, reversibility
DPRK	Democratic People's Republic of Korea
GMR	graphite-moderated reactor
HFO	heavy fuel oil
IAEA	International Atomic Energy Agency
KT	kiloton
LWR	light-water reactor
MIA	missing in action
NPT	Treaty on the Non-Proliferation of Nuclear Weapons
POW	prisoner of war
ROK	Republic of Korea
TPA	tonnes per annum
UN	United Nations
UNSC	United Nations Security Council

CHAPTER ONE

Introduction

In 1994, faced with North Korea's intent to withdraw from the nuclear Non-Proliferation Treaty, the United States negotiated its first agreement with North Korea. The result was the Agreed Framework, an agreement under which North Korea said it would halt its nuclear weapons program immediately in exchange for energy supplies and other assistance over a period of nine years.

That agreement ultimately collapsed over the next eight years, though not without some short-term gains. Twenty-six years and several official dialogues later, the two countries again face rising tension. Without proper management of the North Korean nuclear weapons program, there is a danger of escalating confrontation and even conflict. After two leadership-level dialogues in June 2018 and February 2019, the level of diplomatic dialogue has declined, in terms of both the substantiveness of issues discussed and the seniority of representation.

In this study, we ask whether opportunities for conflict resolution and consensus-building between North Korea and the United States still exist in the current political atmosphere. The purpose of this study is methodological: to explore whether a different framework of negotiations would make a difference. Therefore, we proposed and tested an approach to negotiations that is designed to address the reasons for past failures and that reflects current realities. We term this approach the *portfolio method.*

We found that past negotiations foundered on the lack of agreement on frameworks that could have been reached prior to negotiations on action plans. Using this analysis of past failures, we developed several key elements that should be part of the framework for any new negotiations. Although parts of these elements were present in earlier negotiations, the portfolio method may improve the likelihood of success because it brings together a sufficient number of elements to address the reasons for past failure.

To test the portfolio method, we assembled a team of experts, who went through the steps for portfolio creation with actual cases using the portfolio method and provided a review. We used the method of Track II dialogue to assemble experts with differing national interests to investigate how breakdowns in negotiations can be addressed.[1]

Thus, this project consists of the following steps: (1) develop the portfolio method, (2) apply it to develop test cases, and (3) validate the test cases using experts.

Step One: Develop the Portfolio Method

In the first part of the project, we undertook analyses to support the portfolio method. These analyses included the following:

- An assessment of the causes of past failures in negotiations and their implications for future negotiations. Three principal reasons were identified: (1) disagreements on the goals of negotiations,

[1] Although the assessment methods are similar, our approach differs from Track II diplomacy in one significant respect. Track II diplomacy brings together informed nonstate individuals with differing national interests, with the aim of reaching an agreed position and influencing official views. Because of the authoritarian nature of North Korea, involving nonstate actors from that country has not generally been possible because official diplomats invariably become involved. See Tara Francis Chan, "What Goes on Inside the Secretive, Semi-Official Talks Between the North Korea, the US, and South Korea," *Business Insider*, March 19, 2018. However, we asked experts to consider the issues from all sides, not just their national interest. For more information on Track II diplomacy, see Montville's pioneering work on Track II diplomacy: Joseph V. Montville, "Track Two Diplomacy: The Work of Healing History," *Journal of Diplomacy and International Relations*, Vol. 7, No. 2, Summer/Fall 2006, p. 15. The success record of Track II diplomacy is mixed, but there are some notable successes. See Charles Homans, "Track II Diplomacy: A Short History," *Foreign Policy*, June 20, 2011.

(2) inadequate domestic and international support (both state and nonstate), and (3) the failure to use trust-building mechanisms.
- The development of the key elements of the portfolio method. These are (1) the inclusion of countries with national interests that overlap those of the United States and North Korea, (2) prior agreement on the goals of negotiation between the negotiating parties, (3) the inclusion of primarily hard commitments in agreements, (4) the incorporation of the preferences of in-country stakeholders, (5) the linking of multiple areas of negotiation, and (6) trust-building mechanisms.
- Development of a logic model for the portfolio method that incorporates (1) the countries and their in-country stakeholders and an understanding of the goals and concerns of these stakeholders, (2) the negotiation goals that will be agreed to by all the countries as the basis for negotiating action plans, (3) the constraints that action plans must meet to address goals and concerns, and (4) the action plans and portfolios.

Step Two: Develop Test Cases

Using the logic model, we identified China, South Korea, and the United States as the countries that should be involved in negotiations with North Korea. We also identified the key stakeholders in each of these countries whose support would be needed by the country's political leadership to implement agreements. These were selected from the military, the economic establishment, civil society, and the political opposition, depending on the situation in each country.

We identified three negotiation goals, as follows, with the caveat that each goal needs to be accepted in conjunction with other goals being achieved: (1) improving North Korea's economy, (2) maintaining North Korea's domestic political stability, and (3) improving North Korea's relations with other country stakeholders.

We identified a set of constraints on proposals (action plans[2]) and portfolios as follows: (1) contributes to the negotiation goals, individually and jointly, (2) reciprocity of gains and losses from the portfolio of action plans, (3) implementable in the short-term at low cost, (4) verifiability, and (5) reversibility or low-cost replaceability. We use the acronym CRIVR to denote these constraints.

We proposed several action plans and subjected them to the CRIVR constraints. The 12 action plans that met these constraints were divided into national defense action plans (six), diplomacy action plans (two), economy action plans (two, with several subordinate action plans), and public diplomacy action plans (two). We then mapped the action plans to goals to show which action plan addressed each goal and whether the action plans together addressed all the goals.

Step Three: Validate Through Expert Dialogue

To test the portfolio method, we assembled a team of experts, who went through the steps for portfolio creation with actual cases and provided a review.

One limitation of our test method in comparison with actual negotiations relates to participation: It was not possible to involve non-state actors from North Korea in the dialogue. However, we asked the experts to consider issues from all sides, not just their national interest.

We modified our test method from the typical Track II dialogue to improve its relevance in the following way. The typical role of experts in such dialogues has been to provide analyses, assessments, and recommendations of action plans. In such cases, the role of the research team is to identify a crucial issue, frame a suitable research question on that issue, and assemble a qualified group of experts to discuss the issue. In the portfolio method, the role of experts shifts from the typical three-part role. Instead of reliance on experts for all three tasks, RAND researchers undertake analyses and assessments of action

---

2 Definitions of *action plans* and other terms are in the text of this report and in the glossary at the end of this report.

plans and present them for expert review. The role of experts focuses on reviewing the RAND research and using it as a basis for developing recommendations. The advantage of this approach is that it enables the selection of experts with experience in policymaking rather than the wider range of skills needed in the typical expert dialogue. This is closer to the situation of actual negotiations.

The expert dialogue proceeded as follows. First, the action plans were reviewed for the support they would receive from in-country stakeholders. Only those action plans that passed threshold levels of consensus were considered for final portfolios. Second, experts discussed combinations of action plans that would meet the negotiation goals. Using this discussion, experts proposed three portfolios with different levels of risk, trade-offs, and ongoing commitments. Finally, the expert panel identified the roles that stakeholder countries could play with regard to ensuring that the agreements succeed.

The resultant portfolios are intended to illustrate possible arrangements between North Korea and the United States that (1) exemplify their convergent and divergent interests, (2) suggest how their convergent interests can be enhanced for their mutual benefit, (3) indicate how their divergent interests can be mitigated by reciprocal concessions that, together with item (2), will result in portfolios that both sides view as preferable to present circumstances, and (4) are feasible—i.e., negotiable, verifiable, and sustainable.

The expert dialogue revealed the following:

- The advantages of the portfolio method were (1) prior agreement on the goals of the negotiation, (2) a phased action-for-action set of implementation plans, (3) the inclusion of primarily hard commitments, (4) the incorporation of the preferences of in-country stakeholders, (5) the inclusion of multiple areas of negotiation, and (6) the use of trust-building mechanisms. The disadvantages were (1) the outcomes of the portfolio method were as subject to stress from unexpected external events as other methods and (2) the synergistic value of portfolios—i.e., that the combined portfolio may be better for both sides than the sum of the individual issues, since there may be important interrelationships between the portfolio constituents—did not emerge.

- Experts uniformly welcomed the shift in their typical role from providing analysis, assessment, and recommendations to reviewing RAND-developed analysis and assessments and developing recommendations, because the process provided more depth to the dialogue. However, the proposed action plans in the test cases lacked the detail that is usually part of actual negotiations. For example, proposals on sanctions relief typically contain such details as the dollar value of reliefs. By contrast, the proposals in our research do not offer such a level of detail. However, experts accepted that the objective of the project was to demonstrate an approach rather than to present detailed action plans. They also noted that dialogues between Track II experts typically tended to also lack such detail.[3]

The remainder of this report proceeds as follows:

- In Chapter Two, we describe the approach and methods of this project and develop a logic model.
- In Chapter Three, we apply the logic model through to the development of portfolios of action plans.
- In Chapter Four, we summarize the recommendations and provide concluding comments.

---

[3] In the past, the domains covered were more limited and were not linked. See, for example, the reduction of trade barriers between the United States and North Korea included in the Agreed Framework. U.S. Department of State, Bureau of Arms Control, Verification, and Compliance, "Agreed Framework Between the United States of America and the Democratic People's Republic of Korea," Washington, D.C., October 21, 1994.

Although the Six-Party Talks involving China, Japan, the two Koreas, Russia, and the United States also tried to address concerns outside the nuclear issue by establishing forums for discussion, they did not include specific action plans and did not combine them to balance the countries' interests. U.S. Department of State, Office of the Spokesman, "Initial Actions to Implement Six-Party Joint Statement," Washington, D.C., February 13, 2007.

CHAPTER TWO

Approach

Our approach begins with a discussion of the causes for past failures. We then discuss the countries that should be involved in the negotiations.

Three principal reasons for past failures were identified: (1) disagreements on the goals of negotiations, (2) inadequate domestic and international support (both state and nonstate), and (3) the failure to use trust-building mechanisms, such as phased action-for-action implementation plans.

Disagreements on the Goals of Negotiations

Prior agreement on the goals to be accomplished in the negotiations appears to be critical for success. This does not mean that each side must have the same benefits to be gained from a common goal. These benefits could differ and typically will differ. For instance, consider the goal of improvement of the North Korean economy. For North Korea, the benefit of economic improvement is that it provides more goods and services to its residents. For the United States, the benefit of North Korea's economic improvement is that a basic human right (the right to life) is addressed.

Further, the goal can be conditionally addressed through particular action plans—e.g., development assistance to North Korea could be conditional on denuclearization. Conditionality enables multiple areas to be addressed in a linked fashion, thus enabling both sides to receive gains.

In the absence of agreement of goals, a negotiator could press for their side's interests and objectives at the expense of the other side's interests and objectives. This can lead to failure and has happened in past negotiations. For instance, the United States focused on denuclearization in negotiations with North Korea in 2018–2019. The Democratic People's Republic of Korea (DPRK) leadership saw denuclearization as a threat to its regime. With perceived regime survival at stake, this focus left no room for negotiating on denuclearization.[1]

The impasse could have been avoided by the adoption by both sides of a shared goal in support of regime stability as a prior condition of negotiations. This approach has precedent: In the 1994 Agreed Framework, it was agreed that the United States would provide a formal assurance against nuclear weapons use against North Korea and would restore political relations with North Korea in the short-term—i.e., the United States would negotiate with North Korea without seeking regime change. Agreement on the goals of negotiation was also important for enabling multiple areas to be addressed in a linked fashion. The Agreed Framework listed several areas of agreed action as a result.

By contrast, the United States had a focus on security while the economic and diplomatic domains were of greater importance to the DPRK throughout the two sides' negotiation as part of the Six-Party Talks.[2] This difference of goals, again, appears to have been a key reason for failure.

This difference of goals also prevented the linking of action plans during negotiations. After the second phase of the fourth round of the Six-Party Talks, a key reason for the breakdown in negotiations was that the United States froze $25 million of North Korean assets as part of a more general money-laundering investigation involving a Chinese bank. North Korea demanded the return of these funds, which was

---

[1] Robert L. Gallucci, "Lessons to Be Learned from Negotiating with North Korea," *38 North*, September 17, 2019.

[2] The Six-Party talks included multiple domains, but progress was not evaluated across domains. See Mary Beth D. Nikitin, Emma Chanlett-Avery, and Mark E. Manyin, *Nuclear Negotiations with North Korea: In Brief*, Washington, D.C.: Congressional Research Service, December 4, 2017; Heesun Wee, "How Kim Jong Un Wants to Develop His Economy and Secure His Regime," *CNBC*, June 11, 2018.

refused by the United States on the argument that the financial and nuclear issues were separate.

The differences across past negotiations in goals and areas of negotiation are summarized in Table 2.1.

As Table 2.1 shows, the difference in goals between the United States and North Korea was lower during the 1994 negotiations than during later negotiations. This arguably led to a more comprehensive approach that may have influenced outcomes. As Table 2.2 summarizes, the 1994 negotiations achieved the most significant progress in terms of agreed action plans. The Six-Party Talks and the Singapore Summit set forth several joint declarations of intent, but the lack of agreement on goals appears to have hindered agreement on action plans.

Inadequate Domestic and International Support

Domestic mechanisms must be in place to enable agreements to weather subsequent efforts to undermine them. The problem is that agreements made by the political leadership of a country may need to be approved and implemented by other stakeholders with political power. To improve the chances of stakeholder support, the leadership should not make commitments that are conditional on the support of other significant stakeholders without their involvement.

The Agreed Framework of 1994 failed on this count. Shipments of heavy fuel oil promised to North Korea under the Agreed Framework frequently were delayed because of congressional reluctance to fund such assistance.[3] As U.S. negotiator Robert Gallucci notes, "the Republicans won the [1994] Congressional elections," which were held shortly after the signing of the Agreed Framework. Gallucci notes that "there was a lack of political will to enforce the Agreed Framework. In fact, the complaints coming from North Korea that the United States dragged its feet and reneged have some validity." Similarly, although

[3] See, for example, Robert Gallucci's comments in Frontline, "Examining the Lessons of the 1994 U.S.-North Korea Nuclear Deal," webpage, undated.

Table 2.1
Comparison of Goals and Areas of Negotiation in Past Negotiations and the Portfolio Method

	Agreed Framework, October 21, 1994	Six-Party Talks, Six Rounds, 2003–2007	Singapore Summit, June 2018	Portfolio Method (RAND Research)
U.S. goals	A1. Eliminate DPRK nuclear threat A2. Maintain DPRK regime stability A3. Improve DPRK economy A4. Restore DPRK's geopolitical relations	A1. Eliminate DPRK nuclear threat[a]	A1. Eliminate DPRK nuclear threat A2. Recover POW/MIA remains	A1. Improve DPRK economy A2. Maintain DPRK regime stability A3. Restore DPRK's geopolitical relations
DPRK goals	B1. Improve DPRK economy B2. Maintain DPRK regime stability B3. Restore DPRK's geopolitical relations	B1. Improve DPRK economy B2. Maintain DPRK regime stability B3. Restore DPRK's geopolitical relations	B1. Improve DPRK economy B2. Maintain DPRK regime stability B3. Restore DPRK's geopolitical relations	B1. Improve DPRK economy B2. Maintain DPRK regime stability B3. Restore DPRK's geopolitical relations
Areas of negotiation (categories of action plans)	C1. National defense and security (A1, B2) C2. Diplomatic relations (A2, A4, B3) C3. Economy (A3, B1)	C1. National defense and security (A1, B2) C2. Diplomatic relations (B3) C3. Economy (B1) C4. Public diplomacy (B3)	C1. National defense and security (A1, B2) C2. Diplomatic relations (B3) C3. Economy (B1) C4. Public diplomacy (A2)	C1. National defense and security (A1, B2) C2. Diplomatic relations (B3) C3. Economy (B1) C4. Public diplomacy (B3)

NOTE: MIA = missing in action; POW = prisoner of war.
[a] The United States and Japan pushed for unilateral complete, verifiable, irreversible denuclearization, while China, Russia, and the Republic of Korea (ROK) were agreeable to the North Korean proposal of a phased denuclearization in line with economic and other reliefs.

Table 2.2
Comparison of Areas of Agreement and Joint Declarations in Past Negotiations and the Portfolio Method

	Agreed Framework, October 21, 1994 (Agreements)	Six-Party Talks, Six Rounds, 2003–2007 (Declarations)	Singapore Summit, June 2018 (Declarations)	Portfolio Method (RAND Research)
Agreed action plans and declarations of intent	1. Close GMRs and later dismantle them[a] 2. Provide LWRs in the long term (by 2003) and 500KT of HFO in the short term 3. IAEA inspections 4. DPRK to remain in NPT 5. Restore economic relations 6. Open liaison office, expand to full political relations in long term 7. Assurance by United States against nuclear use 8. Implement DPRK-ROK 1992 Joint Declaration on Denuclearization	4th round declarations (2005): 1. Verifiable denuclearization 2. Affirm 1992 DPRK-ROK declaration 3. DPRK to return to NPT 4. U.S.-ROK declaration on no nuclear weapons in ROK 5. Security guarantee by United States 6. ROK to provide 2 million Kwh energy upon weapons program shutdown. 7. Restore economic and political relations 5th round (phase 2, 2006), Chair's statement: 1. Verifiable denuclearization reaffirmed 5th round declarations (phase 3, February 2007): 1. Shut down Yongbyon and invite IAEA 2. DPRK to receive 50KT of HFO 6th round (Phase 1, March 2007): 1. United States announces it will free $25M of frozen balances of DPRK 6th round declarations (phase 2, September 2007): 1. DPRK agrees to disable nuclear programs and provide a list of program sites 2. United States will remove designation of DPRK as a state sponsor of terrorism 3. US-DPRK people-to-people exchanges 4. Energy assistance to DPRK of 1000KT HFO	1. Restore political relations 2. Peace regime on the Korean Peninsula 3. Denuclearization of the peninsula 4. Recovery of POW/MIA remains	1. Partially dismantle Yongbyon facilities 2. DPRK reduces nuclear stockpile 3. Punggye-ri inspection 4. Reduce U.S.-ROK exercises 5. Infrastructure aid 6. Textile exports 7. Labor exports 8. Exchange programs 9. Positive information campaign

NOTE: GMR = graphite-moderated reactor; HFO = heavy fuel oil; IAEA = International Atomic Energy Agency; KT = kiloton; LWR = light-water reactor; NPT = Treaty on the Non-Proliferation of Nuclear Weapons.
[a] Arms Control Association, "The U.S.-North Korean Agreed Framework at a Glance," fact sheet, last reviewed July 2018.

the Six-Party Talks proposed a comprehensive long-term package that included security, diplomatic, and economic plans, the commitments lacked resilience to external events: They were easily upset by new strategic discord or political factors in both countries.[4] This is a common cause for negotiation failure. Successful resilience requires built-in mechanisms to address vulnerabilities to external events.[5]

Negotiations and agreements are additionally prone to failure from a lack of follow-on support when mixing hard and soft commitments. For example, the Agreed Framework included soft commitments, such as restoring economic and political relations in the long term, that were both ambiguous and outside the Clinton administration's capacity, given the role of the U.S. Senate. William Perry, who was Secretary of Defense at the time of the Agreed Framework, noted while discussing the Senate's unhappiness with its soft commitments that

> the prospects of being able to proceed on the other aspects of the Agreed Framework were nil. That is, we would not be able to get, for example, to go to a peace agreement, to go to opening diplomatic representation with North Korea. That would never would have gotten through the Congress.[6]

Table 2.3 compares the achievements under past negotiations.

Given the lack of trust that has built up because of the failure to meet soft commitments, future negotiations should ideally focus on hard commitments and include soft commitments only if these are likely to be backed by all stakeholders.

---

4 Robert Carlin and John W. Lewis, *Negotiating with North Korea: 1992–2007*, Stanford, Calif.: Center for International Security and Cooperation, Stanford University, January 2008; International Crisis Group, *North Korea: Beyond the Six Party Talks*, Brussels, June 16, 2015; Gallucci, 2019.

5 Stefano Bartolini, *Restructuring Europe: Centre Formation, System Building, and Political Structuring Between the Nation State and the European Union*, Oxford, United Kingdom: Oxford University Press, 2005.

6 Frontline, undated.

Table 2.3
Comparison of Achievements of Past Negotiations

	Agreed Framework, October 21, 1994	Six-Party Talks, Six Rounds, 2003–2007	Singapore Summit, June 2018
Achievements	1. North Korea suspended its existing and planned plutonium enrichment program and allowed IAEA inspections to confirm the suspension. 2. The promised HFO in the short term was partly delivered. The long-term promise of LWRs was not fulfilled. 3. DPRK restarted its nuclear program via uranium enrichment around 2001–2002. 4. The Bush administration's January 2002 Nuclear Posture Review lists the DPRK as a country against which the United States should be prepared to use nuclear weapons, in violation of the Agreed Framework. 5. Talks were discontinued in 2002.	After 4th round, 2nd phase: 1. The United States rejected combining the financial and nuclear issues. 2. The DPRK subsequently tested its first nuclear weapon in 2006. 3. Progress was not evaluated across domains. After 6th round, 1st phase: 1. After China fails to organize funds transfer, Russia agrees to organize $25M frozen funds transfer (June 2007). 2. The DPRK closes Yongbyon in return for having received fuel aid from the ROK. Closure verified by IAEA. After 6th round, 2nd phase: 1. The DPRK issues inventory of sites and programs in November 2007 and asks for aid. 2. The United States claims the list is incomplete and refuses to allow aid. 3. In 2009, DPRK satellite test, 2nd nuclear test, Battle of Daecheong, Six-Party Talks discontinued.	1. April 2018: Inter-Korea summit. 2. May 2018: Before the summit, the DPRK releases three American detainees and destroys the Punggye-ri nuclear test site. 3. July 2018: The DPRK returns POW/MIA remains.

The fact that agreements will have ramifications globally implies that international support is important in addition to ensuring broad domestic stakeholder support. The United Nations (UN) has been a key player for implementing sanctions on North Korea, for example. In the past, other countries have been involved in direct negotiations, most notably during the Six-Party Talks.

Failure to Build Trust

Successful trust-building is usually an incremental, slow process, with action plans that build on each other.[7] As just discussed, both the Agreed Framework and the Six-Party Talks partly failed because of commitments that were later defaulted on, leading to increased mistrust.[8] Negotiations in 2018–2019 to reduce the DPRK's nuclear weapons capacity foundered on the issue of verifiability.[9] U.S. negotiators demanded international verification because they distrusted North Korean assurances. The North Koreans did not agree. Similarly, proposals to reduce sanctions on petroleum imports for civilian use during the 2018–2019 negotiations failed because of the lack of verifiability on the possible diversion of the petroleum to military use.

To address this issue, trust-building mechanisms, such as a phased approach of actions-for-actions and verifiability of action plans, can help. Selecting the right mix of countries with national interests that overlap the interests of both sides to participate in the negotiations can also help build trust.

Table 2.4 summarizes the reasons for past failures.

---

[7] Arvind Parkhe, "Building Trust in International Alliances," *Journal of World Business*, Vol. 33, No. 4, Winter 1998.

[8] Erin Blakemore, "Bill Clinton Once Struck a Nuclear Deal with North Korea," History.com, updated September 1, 2018; Frontline, undated; Gallucci, 2019.

[9] Robert R. King, "North Koreans Want External Information, but Kim Jong-Un Seeks to Limit Access," Center for Strategic and International Studies, May 15, 2019.

Table 2.4
Comparison of the Reasons for Failure of Past Negotiations

	Agreed Framework, October 21, 1994	Six-Party Talks, Six Rounds, 2003–2007	Singapore Summit, June 2018
Reasons for failure	1. Phased approach rejected 2. Multiple options not linked 3. Views of in-country stake-holders ignored 4. Mixing of hard and soft commitments	1. Disagreement on goals 2. Linked multiple options approach considered but not used consistently 3. Phased approach considered but not used consistently	1. Disagreement on goals 2. Phased approach rejected

Using the analysis in this chapter, we summarize the elements of the portfolio method:[10] (1) prior agreement on the goals of negotiation between the negotiating parties, (2) the inclusion of primarily hard commitments in agreements, (3) the incorporation of the preferences of in-country stakeholders, (4) the inclusion of countries with national interests that overlap those of the United States and North Korea, (5) the linking of multiple areas of negotiation, and (6) the incorporation of trust-building mechanisms, such as phased action-for-action implementation plans.

We propose the logic model illustrated in Figure 2.1 as a way to develop the portfolio method. We first identify the countries that should jointly negotiate with North Korea and key stakeholders within each country. We next identify those goals that will be agreed to by all the countries as the basis for negotiating action plans. Third, we propose action plans that will fulfill the goals and meet the tests of hard commitments, resilience, and trust-building. Fourth, we combine action plans into portfolios of action plans. Steps 1 through 3 use

[10] The term *portfolio method* was chosen to reflect the inclusion of components that jointly satisfy the conditions for success. It is derived from the concept of an investment portfolio, the elements of which jointly address the holder's risk and return preferences.

Figure 2.1
Logic Model

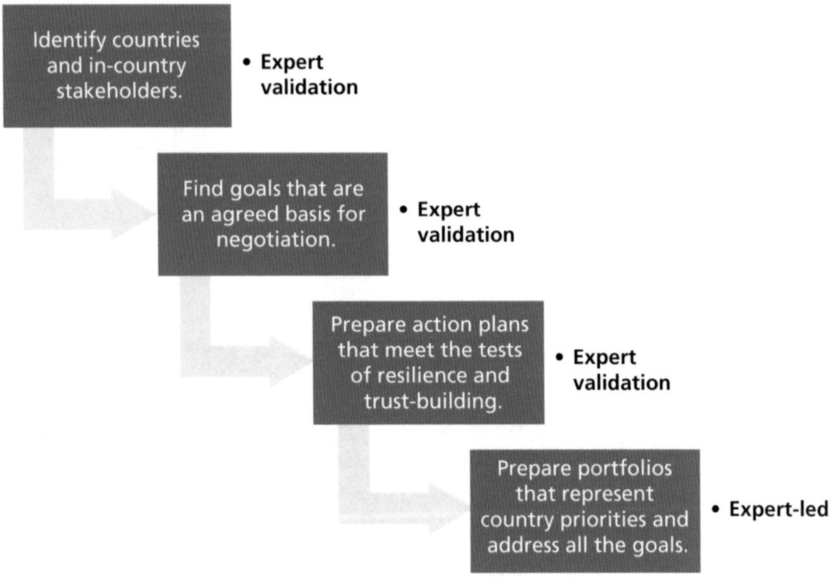

RAND research and are validated through expert assessments. Step 4 is expert-led and uses the results of prior steps.

Discussion of the Logic Model

The logic model shown in Figure 2.1 is intended to provide a way forward by addressing past causes for failure. By explicitly introducing the goals of various parties into the Track II process, the logic model addresses the issue of biases in the goals of negotiations. The portfolio method addresses the issue of a focus on security only, and the inclusion of multiple countries and in-country stakeholders is intended to improve the resilience of agreements. Trust-building is addressed by requiring action plans to meet specific criteria for trust-building, as explained further in the next sections.

Countries

The Six-Party Talks and the DPRK-U.S. 2018–2019 talks showed both the value and the limitations of bringing in more countries to the negotiations. One advantage is that each additional set of stakeholders brings additional interests to the table that could be missed or undervalued if fewer countries participate. This approach also allows for the formation of coalitions for negotiation that increase the bargaining power of weaker players. On the other hand, adding countries can slow negotiations, as the Six-Party Talks demonstrated.[11]

The *current political leadership* (defined as the ruling regime, party, or administration) of each negotiating country is the leading in-country stakeholder. Other in-country stakeholders may also matter if their priorities differ from the political leadership and they can influence outcomes at the stage of implementation. For example, the legislature may have the power to block spending commitments made by the executive,[12] the military and socioeconomic services may be responsible for implementing action plans, and civil society may influence public opinion. It is important to assess the level of consensus of stakeholders behind the political leadership and only accept those action plans for which there is adequate in-country consensus.

For this project, we selected stakeholders from the military, political, economic, and civil society sectors. Not all these groups will be relevant for determining consensus levels for each proposed action. For example, economy stakeholders may not be relevant when establishing

---

[11] International Crisis Group, 2015.

[12] For example, one of the executive commitments of the Clinton administration in the Agreed Framework of October 1994 was to replace the heavy-water reactors then under construction in North Korea with light-water reactor power plants, provided the North Koreans would stop construction and ultimately dismantle the heavy-water reactors. A month later, with the Senate elections of November 1994, the Republican Party won control of the Senate. The Senate made it clear that it would not fund the light-water reactors, regardless of North Korean compliance. In 2001, the country's political leadership changed under the Republican administration of President George W. Bush. The Bush administration defaulted on another provision of the agreement: to supply fuel oil to North Korea to replace the lost fuel from the shutdown of the heavy-water reactors. See U.S. Department of State, Bureau of Arms Control, Verification, and Compliance, 1994; and Blakemore, 2018.

new diplomatic frameworks, and military stakeholders may not be relevant when negotiating sanctions relief.

Goals

Goals refer to the short-term outcomes that countries seek from the negotiations. They include such outcomes as progress toward denuclearization and diplomatic exchanges and exclude long-term outcomes, such as the democratization of the DPRK. There is no clear cutoff between short-term and long-term goals and outcomes. Instead, the difference lies in what can be set out with timelines, such as the destruction of nuclear test sites, and what cannot be set out with timelines, such as democratization. We refer to the short-term goals as *negotiation goals*.

The negotiation goals in the present case should fulfill three conditions. First, they should be consistent with each country's longer-term goals. Second, they should be agreed to by all countries involved in the negotiations. Third, they should be comprehensive and include security, economy, and diplomatic goals.

The first condition is an obvious necessary condition. The logic for the second condition can be understood by what will happen in its absence. As discussed earlier, if countries differ in the outcomes that they want from the negotiations, it will not be possible to develop action plans, since action plans address outcomes. For example, if the DPRK and the United States differ on whether to include proposals for economic development in the negotiations, negotiations will fail. Hence, agreement on negotiation goals is a necessary condition.

The third condition can also be understood by what will happen in its absence. Addressing only a part of the needs of either side could lead to failure. For example, negotiating on economic improvement of the DPRK alone without addressing the external threats the country poses would be unacceptable to the United States. Correspondingly, reducing the external threats posed by the DPRK without economic improvement would be unacceptable to the DPRK.

Note that cross-country agreement on negotiation goals does not necessarily mean that countries agree on long-term goals or on action plans that will fulfill the negotiation goals. For example, the United

States and the DPRK differ on the desirability of democracy as a long-term goal for North Korea. However, the negotiation goal of improving the DPRK's relations with the United States is consistent with both a democratic and an authoritarian North Korea in the long term. Similarly, different countries can and will attach different conditionalities and priorities to the action plans as part of their negotiating package. We discuss this further in the following section.

In past negotiations, the negotiation goals were not explicitly stated. As indicated earlier, differences in goals and priorities regarding goals were important reasons for failure. For these reasons, an immediate challenge for negotiators is to first agree on negotiation goals.

Action Plans

Action plans refer to short-term, timelined courses of action that can be implemented upon the signing of an agreement. Typically, action plans will provide benefits to at least one side and impose costs on at least one side. They should be subject to several constraints. First, and most obvious, they must contribute to the goals individually. Second, the list of agreed action plans should jointly address all the goals agreed to by all sides. Third, the costs and benefits of implementing action plans should be acceptable to all sides. Fourth, they must address goals in a way that builds trust. This not only imposes the condition of verifiability, but also imposes the conditions of reversibility or easy replaceability because it should be possible for other parties to halt, replace, or reverse their commitments if an action plan is not implemented by the responsible party.

Portfolios

Portfolios are combinations of two or more action plans. One reason for considering portfolios over single action plans is, as noted earlier, to avoid the bias toward one's goals—i.e., that different sides are likely to prioritize the same action plan differently. This means that there are few, if any, action plans that all parties will agree should be implemented with the same priority. On the other hand, negotiating portfolios of action plans with different priorities may allow greater scope to find agreement through the netting of gains and losses. As Shifrinson notes, "the key to identifying a settlement is . . . asking whether parties appear to recognize limits to the scope of their competition and seem willing to bargain with one another on the core issues at stake."[13] In short, although there might be no or very few win-win action plans, there could be several win-win portfolios that all parties can commit to.

A second reason for a portfolio approach is that it allows for trading security, diplomatic, and economic components against one another. Although single action plans typically will focus on just one of these three components, a portfolio approach enables the selection of a set of action plans that jointly contribute to all the goals.

We summarize the constraints on action plans and portfolios as follows: (1) contributes to the negotiation goals, individually and jointly, (2) reciprocity of gains and losses from the portfolio of action plans, (3) implementable in the short term, (4) verifiability, and (5) reversibility or low-cost replaceability. We use the acronym CRIVR to denote these constraints.

---

[13] Joshua Shifrinson, "Security in Northeast Asia: Structuring a Settlement," *Strategic Studies Quarterly*, Vol. 13, No. 2, Summer 2019, p. 27.

CHAPTER THREE
Application of the Logic Model

In this chapter, we follow the logic model developed in Chapter Two and illustrated in Figure 2.1.

Country Selection

We identified China, South Korea, and the United States as the countries that will be involved in negotiations with North Korea. We discuss each in turn.

We include China for several reasons. First, as a regional power and a neighbor, China has an interest in the peace and stability on the Korean Peninsula, and North Korea's nuclear weapon and ballistic missile programs are a threat to that peace and stability. Note that China has played a major role in imposing sanctions on North Korea.

Second, China has a role to play in the successful implementation of an agreement. It has a treaty of mutual aid and cooperation with North Korea and is North Korea's closest ally. One condition under which North Korea could denuclearize is if China steps in as guarantor for North Korea's security in the same way that the U.S.-ROK alliance assures South Korea's security.

Third, China is a technologically advanced country and could play a significant role in ensuring the compliance of all sides with agreements.

Fourth, North Korea may be expected, as a peace plan progresses, to receive substantial investment to upgrade its infrastructure and boost its global trade. China is already the world's leading supplier of infrastructure through its Belt and Road Initiative, which it could extend to North Korea. China is North Korea's only substantial trading partner and can play a role in boosting North Korean trade.

South Korea is included because it is the most likely to be involved in any military action in the peninsula (and is thus anxious to avoid conflict), shares ethnic ties with North Korea, could become a major trading partner with the DPRK, and has a desire for reunification with North Korea.

The United States is included because it has been involved in the affairs of the Korean Peninsula since the 1940s, leads the sanctions efforts against North Korea, and has a mutual defense treaty with South Korea. North Korea's progress in developing missiles that could be used against the United States has also increased U.S. interest in a deal with North Korea.

We exclude some stakeholders that are potentially significant. These are Russia, the UN, and Japan. We consider the reasons for their exclusion in turn.

With regard to Russia, it has increasing security concerns arising from North Korea's weaponization program. It also has a broad interest in the DPRK's internal political stability. Both interests coincide with that of the included stakeholder countries. The area in which its interests differ is insulating its economy from the dealmaking process. To this end, it seeks to protect the flow of coal from Russia to China by rail from the Russian border port of Rajin through North Korea and into China. Russia has protected this interest by the insertion of a specific exemption for this activity in successive UN Security Council (UNSC) resolutions.[1] Russia does not have any treaty obligations in the peninsula. As a result, its further interest in resolving the challenges of the Korean Peninsula is limited.

We exclude the UN because China, Russia, and the United States are veto-wielding permanent members of the UNSC. As long as the portfolio of approved action plans protects these countries' interests, the remaining permanent members of the UNSC (Britain and France) will likely go along.

---

[1] UNSC, Resolution 2371 (2017), August 5, 2017a.

Japan is excluded despite significant security interests. Its interests include (1) North Korea's nuclear, chemical, and biological weapons; (2) North Korea's short-, medium-, and long-range missiles; (3) the unresolved issue of abducted Japanese nationals in the 1970s and 1980s;[2] and (4) a weakening of its regional position that would result from portfolios that strengthen intrapeninsular relations or China's relations with South Korea.[3] In addition, Japan's financial resources may be tapped in any deal, as was done in the 1994 Agreed Framework.[4] Japan also has ambitions to be a regional power.

Some of Japan's interests may differ from the main stakeholder countries. In particular, Japan puts a higher priority than its ally the United States on deterring the development of short- and medium-range missiles (part of item 2 above), the abducted Japanese nationals issue (item 3), and the effect of a deal on Japan's influence in the region (item 4).

However, there are two reasons for excluding Japan. First, some of its highest-priority items (item 1 and long-range missiles, included in item 2) coincide with U.S. interests. Hence, Japan can rely on the United States to protect these interests.

Second, despite Japan's efforts to be part of the dealmaking process, such as the trilateral summit that it organized in May 2018 with Chinese and South Korean leadership,[5] the reality is that Japan is not playing a significant role and is not expected to do so in the near term. Instead, it has been relying on the strength of the U.S.-Japan alliance

---

[2] J. Berkshire Miller, "Japan's North Korean Anxieties," *American Interest*, May 15, 2018.

[3] Japan is also potentially an important long-term trading partner for North Korea. In 2000, Japan received 23 percent of North Korea's exports (more than China) and sent 11 percent of North Korea's imports (Observatory of Economic Complexity, "Where Does North Korea Export To?" webpage, undated). The sanctions have obviously changed these relationships in subsequent years.

[4] For the text of the Agreed Framework, see U.S. Department of State, Bureau of Arms Control, Verification, and Compliance, 1994; for Japan's role, see Rachel Blomquist and Daniel Wertz, "An Overview of North Korea-Japan Relations," National Committee on North Korea, updated June 2015.

[5] Tomohiro Osaki, "Japan, China and South Korea Are 'in Sync' on North Korea, Japanese Official Says," *Japan Times*, May 9, 2018.

to have the United States represent its interests and will likely continue to do so.

There is also the concern that the fragile state of bilateral relationships between Japan and South Korea and between Japan and China might lead to a playing out of national interests that are not relevant to the issues at hand. This was believed to have been a factor that adversely affected outcomes at the Six-Party Talks.

This exclusion leaves some of Japan's issues still unaddressed: specifically, the issues of short- and medium-range missiles and abducted nationals. Further, Japan's exclusion from the dealmaking process currently underway will increase its concerns about its regional ambitions.

In-Country Stakeholders

The military establishment is included as a stakeholder in all four countries because it plays a significant role in these countries, albeit to different degrees and in different ways. For example, the military establishment likely influences the political leadership more in North Korea than in China, South Korea, and the United States.[6] This is partly because, unlike China, South Korea, and the United States, many of North Korea's resources are channeled to the military for a variety of reasons, including developing nuclear capabilities and maintaining internal order. Over time, the military has also become a powerful source of patronage. As a result, there is an established military elite in North Korea with a strong voice in policymaking and implementation.

The economic establishment is included as a stakeholder in China, North Korea, and South Korea, but not in the United States. In North Korea, the economic establishment consists of two groups. The first is an established group: the old economy elites, ensconced since the time of Kim Il Sung, who are responsible for controlling the flow of key resources, such as petroleum, rare earth metals, and luxury goods, par-

[6] McEachern shows that several institutions, including the military, shape North Korea's policies. See Patrick McEachern, "North Korea's Policy Process: Assessing Institutional Policy Preferences," *Asian Survey*, Vol. 49, No. 3, May/June 2009.

ticularly through foreign trade.[7] As the market economy has developed more recently, a new group, focusing on trading and often called the *donju*, has come into being. Undoubtedly, both groups survive on the patronage of the political leadership and may not be as distinct as the media sometimes portrays. Still, their motives and preferences could be different. The donju benefit from greater marketization and monetization of the economy, whereas the old economy elites benefit from monopolies and limited marketization and monetization.

Both the old economy elites and the donju can influence policymaking in North Korea. The former derive their power from traditional links to state-owned enterprises and control of foreign trade, through which they can channel resources to the political leadership. The latter derive their power from their role in sustaining the market economy, which has been important for the survival of the current regime.

By contrast, the economies of the other stakeholder countries are highly marketized. This reduces the political importance of economic players. However, South Korea's economic elites, the *chaebol*, could play a significant role through investing in inter-Korean economic initiatives.[8] Hence, they are included as a stakeholder.

In China, state-owned enterprises have historically played a major role in channeling big-ticket exports to North Korea. This role continues, now supplemented by private Chinese enterprises. Hence, Chinese businesses are also included as a stakeholder.

The United States currently has no business interests in North Korea. This may change in the future but is not likely to be outside the market economy. The influence of business interests will, therefore, be limited. Hence, we exclude the economic establishment as a stakeholder in the case of the United States.

---

7 Kook-Yeol Bae, "A Study of the Economic Elites in the Kim Jong-il Era [in Korean]," *Association of North Korean Studies*, Vol. 35, No. 2, December 30, 2010. See also Choe Sang-Hun, "North Korea's State-Run Economy Falters Under Sanctions, Testing Elite Loyalty," *New York Times*, April 18, 2019.

8 Nyshka Chandran, "Seoul Is Relying on Big Companies to Invest in North Korea, so Promised Reforms Are Taking a Backseat," *CNBC*, October 9, 2018.

We have included civil society as a stakeholder in South Korea and the United States. In South Korea's case, this is because civil society's views on North Korea are influential in regard to South Korean policymaking on North Korea. These views concern the full range of issues that affect intrapeninsular relations, including humanitarian issues; people-to-people connectivity in culture, business, and other areas; nuclear threats; and unification.[9] In the United States, civil society's views on North Korea are also important but limited mostly to humanitarian and security issues. However, civil society does not have an effective voice in China or North Korea and is not included among those countries' intranational stakeholders.

Finally, in South Korea and the United States, political opposition parties can influence policymaking on North Korea and are, therefore, included as stakeholders. We also include Congress in the case of the United States because it has lawmaking powers in regard to foreign policy.

Box 3.1 summarizes the list of stakeholders we analyzed in each country. In a real negotiation process, some of these stakeholders are likely to be more influential than others in ways that may be difficult to predict. In a given regime or administration, for example, personal relationships may translate into high levels of influence for leading officials in one of these stakeholder groups in very idiosyncratic ways. The critical first step for this methodology is to identify the range of stakeholders; their specific attitudes and relative influence can be assigned as information allows.

We now turn to discussing the goals.

Getting to Agreed Negotiation Goals

We start by proposing the negotiation goals of North Korea. Earlier, we discussed three conditions that the goals must fulfill. First, they

[9] Lenka Kudláčová, "South Korean Civil Society Organizations as Confidence-Builders? The Experience with South Korean Civil Society Groupings in the Republic of Korea and the DPRK," *Perspectives*, Vol. 22, No. 2, 2014.

Box 3.1
List of In-Country Stakeholders, by Country

China
- Political leadership
- Military
- Businesses

ROK
- Political leadership
- Military
- Political opposition
- Civil society

DPRK
- Political leadership
- Military
- Economy elites
- Donju

United States
- Political leadership
- Military
- Political opposition
- Congress
- Civil society

should be consistent with each country's longer-term goals. Second, they should be agreed to by all countries involved in the negotiations. Third, they should be comprehensive, rather than partial, regarding the needs of the situation. In the present case, this means that the goals should be comprehensive regarding the state of the DPRK. They should, therefore, cover both economic issues and diplomatic relations in addition to national security.

The proposed long-term goals of the negotiating countries are listed in Table 3.1. There are six goals. The first four goals address domestic issues, and the last two goals address external relations.

The assignments of national preferences in Table 3.1 ("for" and "against" each option) are admittedly generic and binary. Clearly, individual actors and organizations within each country will have different views on each of these options. No country, as a comprehensive decisionmaking body, will be wholly for or against any one of them. These initial, simple assessments reflect the best overall judgment, according to our research. They are provisional and illustrative of the methodology rather than final determinations; a more-developed model could produce more-graduated and more-nuanced assessments.

For example, although all sides favor a nuclear-free peninsula, there are differences in the interpretation of this state. For China and North Korea, a nuclear-free peninsula includes both North and South

Table 3.1
Long-Term Goals Regarding North Korea

Country	Economic Development	Autocracy	Domestic Power-Sharing	Democracy	Nuclear-Free Peninsula	Unification
China	For	Against	For	Against	For	For
North Korea	For	For	Against	Against	For	For
South Korea	For	Against	For	For	For	For
United States	For	Against	For	For	For	For

Korea.[10] For the United States and South Korea, this means a nuclear-free North Korea.[11]

There is also a difference between sides on how North Korea ought to approach nuclearization in the context of economic growth. Faced with what it sees as an existential threat, North Korea has pursued both nuclearization and economic growth in recent years, particularly under Kim Jong Un's marketization initiatives. This dual-development policy, also termed the *byungjin policy*, should be no surprise, since nuclearization is impossible to sustain without financial resources. However, the United States and the international community have posed nuclearization as a choice for which North Korea must pay an economic price.

As Table 3.1 shows, the countries' long-term goals are not all in agreement with one another. Those agreed on are economic development, a nuclear-free peninsula, and unification. Of these goals, negotiating unification appears to be the least likely to be successful without prior progress on other long-term goals, such as governance systems (autocracy, domestic power-sharing, and democracy). Unification is additionally challenged by the stark differences in economic conditions

---

[10] Scott A. Snyder, "The Motivations Behind North Korea's Pursuit of Simultaneous Economic and Nuclear Development," *Asia Unbound*, Council on Foreign Relations blog, November 20, 2013.

[11] I am grateful to one of the reviewers of this report for this and the subsequent example.

between the two Koreas. Hence, we ruled out unification as a basis for deriving negotiation goals.

The other two long-term goals are retained because they are the most important priorities of North Korea (economic development) and the United States (denuclearization). Hence, we select negotiation goals that derive from these two long-term goals.

We evaluated the following negotiation goals that are consistent with economic development and denuclearization.

Proposed Negotiation Goal 1: Improving North Korea's Economy

This goal is consistent with each country's long-term goal for North Korea's economic development. In reality, there are many exceptions and qualifications to this judgment: The United States, for example, only endorses this goal when accompanied by significant nonproliferation agreements and North Korean foreign and domestic reforms. But we believe that it is accurate to say that, with the right qualifications, all the stakeholders agree that economic development in North Korea can contribute to their preferences.

Proposed Negotiation Goal 2: Maintaining North Korea's Domestic Political Stability

For different countries, the DPRK's domestic political stability offers different long-term benefits. For the current leadership of the DPRK, it can sustain autocracy under the current regime. For China, it is an interim step toward achieving a power-sharing regime under authoritarian rule.[12]

The United States and the ROK prefer a democratic North Korea in the long term. A peaceful regime change toward democracy is, therefore, preferred by the United States and the ROK over the current regime. However, the alternative to the current regime could also be an unstable, nuclear-armed regime. The status quo, characterized by

---

12 China allegedly supported a coup attempt by Kim's uncle and half-brother. See Katherine Lam, "Kim Jong Un Killed Uncle, Half-Brother over 'China Coup Plot,' Report Says," *Fox News*, updated September 25, 2017.

a strong leader with the power to fulfill agreements without domestic turmoil, is better than that outcome.

In the past, the United States and the ROK have made assurances about building long-term diplomatic relations with the incumbent regime, as discussed earlier. Hence, we infer that this is a generally agreed negotiation goal.

Proposed Negotiation Goal 3: Improving North Korea's Relations with the Other Three Countries

This goal has been a feature of the Agreed Framework, the Six-Party Talks, and the Singapore Summit. It is critical for deriving action plans that improve the security situation in the peninsula, such as reducing North Korea's nuclear capabilities.

Proposed Negotiation Goal 4: Improving Human Rights in North Korea

We take an approach that is common in the literature and view the improvement of human rights as part of the long-term goal of democratization.[13] Hence, this negotiation goal addresses democratization. However, as just argued, democratization is inconsistent with the long-term goal of the DPRK leadership. In the past, the United States has been willing to exclude human rights from the negotiation agenda despite its concerns about human rights in the DPRK.[14] Therefore, we do not include this goal in the list of pre-agreed negotiation goals.

With regard to the three agreed negotiation goals, the political leaderships of the external stakeholder countries have, at various times, endorsed all these goals, even though their priorities among the goals have differed.[15] The three goals also fulfill the third condition, laid

---

[13] See Laza Kekic, "The Economist Intelligence Unit's Index of Democracy," *The Economist*, 2007; and Laurence Whitehead, "Democratization and Human Rights in the Americas: Should the Jury Still Be Out?" in Louise Fawcett and Mónica Serrano, eds., *Regionalism and Governance in the Americas: Continental Drift*, London: Palgrave Macmillan, 2005.

[14] Human rights was not on the agenda of the negotiations for the Agreed Framework of 1994, the Six-Party Talks, or the Singapore Summit.

[15] See White House, "Joint Statement of President Donald J. Trump of the United States of America and Chairman Kim Jong Un of the Democratic People's Republic of Korea at

out earlier, of meeting all the needs of the DPRK—i.e., domestic and external needs.

We now turn to the selection of action plans.

Selecting Action Plans

We considered several action plans for inclusion. We divided the action plans into four categories: national defense, diplomacy, economy, and public diplomacy. In this section, we discuss only those action plans that meet the CRIVR constraints discussed earlier. The full list, along with the CRIVR screening, is provided in Appendix A.

National Defense Action Plans

The list of national defense action plans that passed the CRIVR analysis is as follows:

1. The DPRK partially dismantles its Yongbyon nuclear facilities, under international inspection.
2. The DPRK reduces its nuclear stockpile by destroying a certain number of warheads.
3. The DPRK reduces its conventional military capacity.
4. The DPRK allows international inspectors to examine the destroyed Punggye-ri nuclear test site.
5. The United States and ROK reduce major military exercises.[16]
6. The United States and ROK reduce military capability on the peninsula.

---

the Singapore Summit," Singapore, June 12, 2018; Isabella Steger, "North and South Korea Agreed to Work on Formally Ending the Korean War," *Quartz*, April 27, 2018; and Keegan Elmer, "Chinese President Xi Jinping Gives North Korean Leader Kim Jong-Un His Full Support," *South China Morning Post*, June 19, 2019.

[16] North Korea could also reduce its military exercises. We have not considered this possibility further in this report. Also, as noted earlier, there could be levels of detail that enable negotiations to be more nuanced. For example, military exercises could be reduced rather than stopped completely.

National defense action plans are divided into two categories: (1) action plans that reduce the external threat from North Korea and (2) action plans that reduce the external threat to North Korea.

The action plans that reduce the threat from the DPRK are as follows:

1. The DPRK partially dismantles its Yongbyon nuclear facilities, under international inspection.
2. The DPRK destroys a certain number of warheads.
3. The DPRK reduces its conventional military capacity.
4. The DPRK allows international inspectors to examine the destroyed Punggye-ri nuclear test site.

The main difference between the four action plans is their impact on long-term nuclear capacity. Although none critically impair the DPRK's long-term capacity to produce nuclear weapons, reducing conventional military capacity will have the least impact. Allowing international inspection at Punggye-ri will have low impact, since the site has allegedly been at least partly destroyed.[17] Destroying a certain number of warheads will more greatly affect long-term capacity, while partially dismantling Yongbyon's nuclear facilities could have the most negative impact on long-term capacity.

To improve relations externally, North Korea would prefer to maintain some of its nuclear weapons and delivery capabilities as ways to coerce other countries into dealing with it. South Korea and the United States favor denuclearization and missile decommissioning as ways to improve inter-Korea relations and U.S. security. China has favored a nuclear-free North Korea as well, fearing that it raises the chance of inter-Korean war, which would invariably affect China.

In the 2019 Hanoi meetings between Donald Trump and Kim Jong Un, the discussions were critically affected by the U.S. claim that there were additional undisclosed sites beyond Yongbyon. The same situation arose during the Six-Party Talks. As part of the agreements at

---

[17] See, for example, "North Korea Nuclear Test Tunnels at Punggye-ri 'Destroyed,'" *BBC*, May 24, 2018.

the end of the second phase of the sixth round of the Six-Party Talks, the DPRK agreed to provide an inventory of its nuclear program (both development and test sites) and did so. The United States claimed that the site list was incomplete, leading to the permanent discontinuation of those talks.

The expert panel felt that a list of sites was not needed, since it would not be agreed on by both sides. Instead, a partial dismantlement of Yongbyon would be evidence of incremental progress that could be agreed to by both sides.

For North Korea, nuclearization has been critical to achieving the goal of assuring its safety and regime survival from perceived threats by the United States and the U.S.-ROK alliance. Although North Korea has committed to long-term denuclearization,[18] short-term action plans that reduce its nuclear capabilities significantly would threaten the goal of external safety in the short term. Nevertheless, the political leadership of North Korea could consider reductions to reduce its capacity in the short term rather than cause long-term damage to its nuclear capacity if they are suitably calibrated with reductions in U.S.-originated capabilities that it perceives as threats to its security.[19] Among in-country stakeholders, the DPRK military may consider the situation somewhat differently from the political leadership. For instance, it may be concerned about the adverse effect on the resources made available to the military in the event of a reduction in the DPRK's military capability.

For the United States and ROK, North Korea's nuclear program is perceived to be a major threat to their security, and therefore both countries would be interested in action plans that reduce the DPRK's nuclear capability.[20] Both countries would likely favor a reduction in North Korea's conventional military capacity, although the conven-

---

[18] See, for example, Uri Friedman, "What Does 'Denuclearization' Mean to Kim Jong Un?" *The Atlantic*, March 28, 2018.

[19] The DPRK leadership does not and would not explicitly state this consideration. However, it follows from North Korea's perception that its nuclear weapons are its main protection from a U.S. threat. See Bruce Klingner, "Why Does North Korea Want Nukes?" Heritage Foundation, August 13, 2018.

[20] See, for example, U.S. Office of the Director of National Intelligence, *Worldwide Threat Assessment of the U.S. Intelligence Community*, Washington, D.C., February 13, 2007.

tional arms balance has arguably shifted in favor of the ROK in recent years.[21]

China's political leadership views the removal of North Korea's nuclear program as a desirable outcome but does not see North Korea's nuclear weapons as an immediate threat to its security.[22] China's preference, accordingly, will likely be positive but of lower priority than that of the United States or ROK.

The action plans that reduce the threat to the DPRK are as follows:

1. The United States and ROK reduce major military exercises.
2. The United States and ROK reduce military capability on the peninsula.[23]

We have proposed two action plans under this subcategory. With regard to reducing the threat to the DPRK, a partial halt to major field exercises is in effect as of this writing. The second action plan, reducing military capacity, is a short-term action plan that could take several forms, such as reducing troop deployments to forward positions or mothballing some equipment.

North Korea likely views both action plans as important. Although the second plan reduces the potential threat, the first removes an immediate threat because the DPRK believes that major military exercises can disguise an actual assault.[24]

South Korea's views on the two plans may differ from those of the United States, particularly among in-country stakeholders. South

---

[21] Adam Mount, *Conventional Deterrence of North Korea*, Washington, D.C.: Federation of American Scientists, 2019.

[22] Andrew Scobell, "China and North Korea: Bolstering a Buffer or Hunkering Down in Northeast Asia?" testimony presented before the U.S.-China Economic and Security Review Commission on June 8, 2017, Santa Monica, Calif.: RAND Corporation, CT-477, 2017.

[23] North Korea could also reduce its military exercises. We have not considered this possibility further in this report.

[24] See, for example, Dagyum Ji, "Seoul 'Must Stop' Joint U.S.-ROK Military Drills: DPRK Media," *NK News*, January 11, 2018; and Chad O'Carroll, "Military Drills Will Lead to 'Unimaginable Holocaust,' Says N. Korea," *NK News*, January 16, 2014.

Korea's political leadership is likely to view these plans as negotiable in return for gains elsewhere, similar to the views of the United States. These gains could be in national security as well as in public diplomacy. However, unlike the United States, the ROK's military and political opposition will likely oppose these plans regardless of gains elsewhere. The military may be particularly concerned about the effect of these action plans on the preparedness of the ROK military and the U.S.-ROK alliance. The political will to implement agreements to reduce conventional military preparedness through these two action plans in the ROK might, therefore, be lower than in the United States.

Because these action plans do not have direct economic implications, we do not include economic stakeholders in this analysis.

Diplomacy Action Plans

We consider two diplomacy action plans:

1. The United States and DPRK establish liaison offices.
2. An end-of-war declaration.

The United States and DPRK Establish Liaison Offices

Liaison offices are representative offices of a country in another country with which it does not have full diplomatic relations. They are primarily confidence-building measures on the path to establishing full diplomatic relations. Liaison offices have limited purposes by themselves and might not, for example, issue visas or negotiate agreements on national security, trade, or other areas in the way that a full embassy can. They primarily are channels of communication located in the partner country.

At the time of the last initiative by the United States and DPRK to establish liaison offices in 1995, which was subsequent to the 1994 Agreed Framework, intense discussions between the United States and DPRK were held, and significant progress was made, including an agreed method to set up the offices. At the last minute, the DPRK withdrew from the proposed arrangements.

The fact that a liaison office was not finally agreed to by the DPRK remains a puzzle. The role of the ROK appears to be limited, though not fully absent. It appears that the 1995 negotiations were bilateral, between the United States and DPRK. Negotiations between the ROK and DPRK on the nuclear issue had broken down by the end of 1992, after an agreement earlier in the year to end nuclear weapons development and conduct inspections. The 1994 Agreed Framework was partly initiated to bring the DPRK back to the negotiating table with the ROK. However, in response to the DPRK's apparent willingness to go beyond the 1992 agreement, the Agreed Framework established a broader scope of relationship-building between the United States and DPRK, including envisioning the establishment of liaison offices between the two countries. The ROK initially objected to this as a step too far but was apparently overruled by the United States.[25] This objection does, however, indicate that the ROK was consulted by the United States during this exercise.

It is interesting to speculate why liaison offices between the DPRK and ROK, in existence from September 2018 to June 2020 and believed to be successful (or at least very active), were not envisaged under the Agreed Framework.[26] Presumably, both the DPRK and the United States would have recognized the lower political risks to the DPRK of first establishing a liaison office with the ROK, with liaison offices with the United States being a second step. However, the United States might have seen the establishment of liaison offices with the DPRK as a necessary step in the DPRK's denuclearization and was unwilling to agree to something less (in the U.S. view), such as liaison offices between the ROK and DPRK.

---

[25] Lynn Turk, "North Korea: Liaison Offices—the First Time," *38 North*, June 29, 2018.

[26] These offices were established following the Moon-Kim summit in September 2018 and operated until June 2020, except for a short shutdown of three days by the DPRK in March 2019, perhaps related to the failure of the Hanoi Summit. In June 2020, North Korea demolished the liaison office building as part of a broader move to cut channels of communication with South Korea over anti-DPRK propaganda campaigns emanating from South Korea–based defectors from the DPRK. See Anthony Kuhn, "In 'Terrific Explosion,' North Korea Blows Up Liaison Office," *National Public Radio*, June 16, 2020.

The ROK and DPRK had 285 meetings in the first 100 days after establishing liaison offices. However, the gains from these meetings, if any, are not public knowledge. See Colin Zwirko, "286 Meetings Held at Inter-Korean Liaison Office Since September: MOU," *NK News*, December 20, 2018.

The 2018 Singapore Summit between the United States and DPRK noted the desire of both sides to establish new relations. Although a liaison office was not actively discussed then, it became a topic for informed discussion in the run-up to the 2019 Hanoi Summit.

An End-of-War Declaration

In April 2018, the summit meeting at Panmunjom between Presidents Kim Jong Un and Moon Jae In resulted in an agreement to declare a formal end to the 1950–1953 Korean War, currently in a state of truce.[27] The Trump-Kim summit in June 2018 reaffirmed the agreement. With no opposition from China or other external states, the declaration remains a matter of bilateral agreement between the United States and North Korea.

The two diplomacy action plans discussed in this section primarily address the goal of improving the DPRK's external relations. We include the military and civil society as stakeholders but exclude economic interests. The main difference between the two action plans is in the chance of future conflict in the near term versus the long term. An end-of-war declaration sends a more powerful signal that the chances of near-term conflict are low, whereas a liaison office can play an important role in resolving near-term and long-term tensions. The ROK is likely to support both action plans for these reasons.

Both action plans can bolster the status of the political leadership of the DPRK domestically and can thus improve the regime's legitimacy and domestic stability. This aspect may be opposed by some elements of South Korean civil society and by the South Korean opposition parties.

For North Korea, both action plans reduce the risk of conflict and improve the regime's domestic and external legitimacy. Other countries are likely to be supportive, though perhaps with lower priority than in the DPRK. The United States and, to a lesser extent, the ROK would like to use it more as a concession to be made to the

---

[27] The truce or armistice was signed on June 27, 1953, by North Korea (also representing China) and the United States. South Korea, which refused to accept the division of Korea, was not a signatory.

DPRK in return for gains elsewhere, than for any real effects on reducing the chances of conflict.

Economy Action Plans

We consider two categories of action plans:

1. Trade sanctions relief for the DPRK. We consider this category across a variety of the main items that are currently under sanctions.
2. Provide infrastructure aid to North Korea. This includes short-term action plans, such as revitalizing the special economic zones in the DPRK near the border with South Korea (Kaesong Industrial Zone) and near the Russian and Chinese borders, such as the Rason Special Economic Zone; improving the electricity grid; and restoring existing rail and road links between North and South Korea.

The DPRK economic development framework is the progressive marketization for basic consumer goods and services (such as food and transport) and labor exports—i.e., to expose more of such goods to free domestic and international trade.[28] The country is also looking for foreign capital to build its infrastructure.[29]

These factors explain the two action plans noted in this section. Trade sanctions relief is one key action plan under the goal of economic improvement. For the DPRK, trade sanctions relief may also improve domestic political stability. For example, relief on labor exports improves the regime's legitimacy among the masses, and luxury goods imports improves the regime's legitimacy among economic elites.

Economic sanctions have become more stringent over time. We show this in Table 3.2. Initially covering only items related to nuclear

---

[28] Hyung-Gon Jeong, Byung-Yeon Kim, and Suk Lee, *The Current Situation of Marketization in North Korea and Prospects for Change of Its Economic System*, Seoul: Korea Institute for International Economic Policy, World Economy Update13-10, 2013.

[29] Wee, 2018.

and ballistic weapons development, the sanctions were later modified to cover livelihood goods and services and investment goods.

The impact of sanctions has been dramatic, particularly in 2018, as Tables 3.3 and 3.4 show.

Our discussion covers the leading exports and imports of the DPRK as well as financial flows. The traded items we consider are exports of coal, metals (including minerals), textiles and labor, and imports of petroleum. Our criterion for inclusion is that the trade should be at least 10 percent of total exports or imports in the peak year in Tables 3.3 and 3.4. We include labor exports, which are not listed in Table 3.3 because data on labor exports (remittances) are not available, but estimates suggest that they ranged from $200 million to $500 million a year prior to sanctions.[30]

Within the DPRK, the economic elites, who channel resources through state-owned enterprises and financial flows and import luxury goods for the leadership, are likely to be an important in-country stakeholder. A more recent economic group, the *donju*, has emerged over the past decade. Its membership overlaps with the elites, but not entirely so, and the group is important for the development of the market economy and has helped make markets for common goods (food, apparel, some capital goods) more efficient. The donju are also likely to be an important in-country stakeholder.

China and the ROK's business sectors could be significant actors in any liberalization of the economy, particularly for capital goods, infrastructure development, and consumer goods. Civil society in the ROK, which has emerged as a champion for the rights of lower-income groups in the DPRK, is likely to be interested in sanctions relief on textiles and labor exports and humanitarian-related items, such as petroleum imports. It will also likely support freer financial flows in order to enable remittances.

---

[30] Human Rights First, "North Korean Workers Earn Millions for Their Government Overseas," October 31, 2017. Other estimates go as high as $2.3 billion. Scott A. Snyder, "Human Rights Conditions of Overseas Laborers from North Korea," *Asia Unbound*, Council on Foreign Relations blog, May 22, 2015.

Table 3.2
Summary of DPRK Economic Sanctions

Sanctions	UNSC Resolution 2094 (2013)	UNSC Resolution 2270 (2016)	UNSC Resolution 2321 (2016)	UNSC Resolution 2371 (2017)	UNSC Resolution 2375 (2017)	UNSC Resolution 2397 (2017)
Finance	For weapon development	All	N/A	N/A	N/A	N/A
Livelihood trade: exports	N/A	Rare earths, precious metals	Copper, nickel, silver, and zinc. Ceiling on coal of 7.5 million TPA	Coal, iron ore, seafood, and lead	Textiles	Primary products, capital goods
Livelihood trade: imports	N/A	Freight services	N/A	N/A	Ceiling on petroleum at 2 million TPA and on crude oil at prior year levels	Capital goods, metals, and vehicles. Ceiling on petroleum at 70,000 TPA and on crude oil at 525,000 TPA
Scientific exchange	N/A	All	N/A	N/A	N/A	N/A
People exports	N/A	N/A	N/A	N/A	N/A	All, by end of 2019

SOURCES: Financial Action Task Force, *International Standards on Combating Money Laundering and the Financing of Terrorism & Proliferation*, Paris, updated June 2019; UNSC, Resolution 2094 (2013), March 7, 2013; UNSC, Resolution 2270 (2016), March 2, 2016a; UNSC, Resolution 2321 (2016), November 30, 2016b; UNSC, 2017a; UNSC, Resolution 2375 (2017), September 11, 2017b; UNSC, Resolution 2397 (2017), December 22, 2017c.

NOTE: TPA = tonnes per annum. We exclude trade bans for nonlivelihood purposes. UNSC resolutions for 2013–2016 were passed during the Obama administration. Subsequent UNSC resolutions were during the Trump administration. UNSC Resolution 2321 (2016) imposed a value limit on coal exports of $400 million per year. All ceilings are for annual amounts.

Table 3.3
North Korea's Leading Exports (US$ millions)

Export	2011	2012	2013	2014	2015	2016	2017	2018
Food and agricultural products	131.5	141.5	178.7	287.2	193.0	273.5	282.4	15.1
Minerals, earth, stone, wood, and ceramics	1,684.2	1,669.5	1,911.1	1,607.8	1,373.1	1,485.1	667.1	55.4
Textiles	477.1	487.1	637.7	795.0	837.4	755.6	594.1	8.1
Metals, including precious metals	285.8	231.8	219.0	218.9	105.5	133.9	82.0	36.9
Machinery and electrical equipment	77.7	160.6	107.4	117.0	79.7	72.6	56.4	13.3
Coal	1,174.9	1,247.7	1,423.8	1,173.1	1,081.1	1,190.9	411.1	0.0[a]
Petroleum and petroleum products	97.1	63.5	143.9	17.0	69.6	38.1	9.3	3.7
Total	3,939.3	4,013.7	4,638.3	4,231.6	3,759.3	3,949.8	2,102.3	132.4

SOURCES: Korean Statistical Information Service, homepage, undated; United Nations, "UN Comtrade Database," webpage, undated.

[a] Zero values could indicate unreported trades.

Table 3.4
North Korea's Leading Imports (US$ millions)

Import	2011	2012	2013	2014	2015	2016	2017	2018
Nuclear reactors, boilers, and machinery	307.2	326.3	318.6	329.0	263.4	282.9	272.2	8.4
Vehicles and parts	231.9	240.6	255.9	231.3	197.9	260.6	204.0	2.0
Metals	221.5	230.8	269.8	262.1	245.9	271.6	222.8	5.4
Coal	53.0	58.1	43.2	53.1	53.0	68.5	47.2	0.0[a]
Petroleum and petroleum products	748.7	774.1	800.1	360.4	141.0	120.7	71.1	21.3
Total	1,566.1	1,633.7	1,691.8	1,239.8	905.0	1,008.2	821.1	37.1

SOURCES: Korean Statistical Information Service, homepage, undated; United Nations, "UN Comtrade Database," webpage, undated.

[a] Zero values may indicate unreported trades.

Public Diplomacy Action Plans

We propose the following public diplomacy action plans:

1. People-to-people exchanges: Initiate a public diplomacy program between (1) the DPRK and (2) the ROK and United States for cultural and sports exchanges and academic and scientific exchanges.[31]
2. Initiate a public diplomacy program between (1) the DPRK and (2) the ROK and United States for positive information campaigns on all sides. The program should target domestic and external populations on all sides.[32]

These public diplomacy action plans are of two types: cultural, educational, and professional exchanges and information campaigns, such as international broadcasting initiatives.

Cultural, educational, and professional exchanges include foreign musical concerts, friendly sports matches, and joint participation in the Olympic Games. Professional exchanges (more specifically, scientific and academic exchanges) can have tangible short-term in addition to long-term impacts. These include student exchanges and collaboration on a health care or science project. People-to-people exchanges in hostile political environments with no official diplomatic channel can sometimes be the only channels for the exchange of information and trust- and relationship-building. However, arguably the most effective cultural and professional exchanges are the ones that are consistent, continuous, and well-aligned with foreign policies. That said, each of the three countries analyzed in this report have their own short- to mid-term objectives to consider when pursuing public diplomacy, and these objectives are considered for this report.

International broadcasting efforts, such as Voice of America and British Broadcasting Corporation programming, have been around for many decades. However, the speed, reach, and diversity of communica-

---

[31] Military-to-military exchanges could also be a part of such public diplomacy programs.

[32] These programs can be measured through frame analysis of major news and media platforms and by reviewing the budget allocations for international broadcasting.

tion channels today have expanded the horizon. Media representation of any topic, such as North Korean policies, may be positive or negative even without direct correlation to the DPRK's actions or behavior and could be solely based on a government's foreign policy toward the DPRK. This may be a particularly important factor for democracies or in a highly divided political climate, because information campaigns can target both domestic and foreign audiences to shape public opinion in favor of or against certain foreign policy decisions. For this report, we are focusing only on government-funded news and entertainment broadcasting efforts by the U.S. and ROK governments that target the DPRK.

The stakeholders in each country are assumed to be the political establishment and, for the United States and ROK, civil society. Military and economic interests are excluded because they are unlikely to have a stake in this domain.[33]

These two action plans address confidence-building between countries and thus contribute to external stability. The main difference between these plans, in reference to the long-term goals, is the impact on the DPRK population. Historically, this population has been relatively isolated from the outside world, giving both those within the DPRK and those outside a distorted view of each other's populations.

Media campaigns can have a large footprint and involve a somewhat higher risk for the domestic legitimacy of the DPRK political leadership. This action plan thus comes with a risk to the DPRK political leadership, given the history of past negative information campaigns and the difficulty in controlling information that is widely broadcast. On the other hand, this plan will build confidence among the external stakeholders.

Some people-to-people exchanges, such as a sports encounter or a cultural performance, can also have a large footprint. However, these encounters expose elites to one another and are more easily controlled

---

[33] Military-to-military exchanges, both at the highest levels and at the working level (including visits to bases) could be a possibility down the road. A further step could be joint participation in multilateral exercises and activities that address a common area. However, these two options are unlikely to be part of the first steps because they require a building up of trust.

by the political leadership. Hence, these exchanges can improve the domestic legitimacy of the DPRK political leadership.[34] Further, some people-to-people exchanges, such as those in a scientific context, may support economic stability.

The stakeholders in other countries will largely see both action plans as confidence-building measures and worthy of at least moderate support. The ROK political leadership will be strongly in favor of both action plans, as witnessed by its strong support for the DPRK's participation in the Winter 2018 Olympic Games.

Mapping Action Plans to Goals

Table 3.5 maps the action plans to the goals they are intended to achieve for one or more stakeholders.

All the national defense and diplomacy action plans in Table 3.5 contribute to a single goal (improving external relations). This shows the risks of focusing too narrowly on security issues and highlights the importance of creating portfolios of action plans that include plans that address other goals.

The economy action plans will influence domestic political stability as well. The DPRK's impoverished economy has made it vulnerable to domestic dissent, requiring a heavy clampdown by its leadership to maintain domestic stability. Improving the economy will, therefore, contribute to internal stability.

The public diplomacy action plans directly contribute to external relations and indirectly benefit domestic stability because they will improve the interaction of DPRK residents with the outside world, which appears to be important to many of its residents.[35]

---

[34] Daniel J. Wakin and Sheryl Gay Stolberg, "North Koreans Welcome Symphonic Diplomacy," *New York Times*, February 27, 2008.

[35] King, 2019.

Table 3.5
Mapping Action Plans to Goals for the DPRK

Action Plan	Improve the Economy	Maintain Domestic Political Stability	Improve External Relations
Partially dismantle Yongbyon facilities			X
Destroy some warheads			X
Punggye-ri inspection			X
Reduce DPRK conventional capability			X
Reduce U.S.-ROK exercises			X
Reduce U.S.-ROK military capability			X
Liaison office			X
End-of-war declaration			X
Trade sanctions relief	X	X	
Infrastructure aid	X	X	
Exchange programs		X	X
Positive information campaign		X	X

Recommended Action Plans and Portfolios

We relied on expert dialogue for our recommendation of which action plans to include in the portfolios and the composition of the portfolios. Given the large number of feasible action plans, we asked the experts to consider developing a smaller set of action plans that would fulfill the negotiation goals and be acceptable to country negotiators. Toward this goal, experts ranked the action plans within each category. The outcome of this exercise is shown in Table 3.6.

Regarding the national defense category, experts agreed that the main differences among the four action plans to be implemented by the DPRK related to their impact on long-term nuclear capacity. The ranking in Table 3.6 captures their assessment of the order of impor-

Table 3.6
Expert-Ranked Action Plans

Rank	National Defense	Economy	Diplomacy	Public Diplomacy
1	Partially dismantle Yongbyon	Provide infrastructure aid	United States and DPRK establish liaison offices	People-to-people exchanges
2	DPRK reduces nuclear stockpile	Textile exports	End-of-war declaration	Positive information campaigns
3	United States and ROK reduce major military exercises	Labor exports		
4	Inspections of Punggye-ri	Coal exports and metal exports		
5	DPRK reduces conventional capacity	petroleum imports, science and technology imports, and luxury goods imports		
6	United States and ROK reduce conventional capacity			

tance of the plans. The reduction of U.S. and ROK major military capacity was seen as more important to the DPRK than a reduction of the two countries' conventional capacity.

Regarding the economy category, the ranking reflected the experts' assessment of what would be acceptable to all sides. Although coal and metal exports were the most important from a DPRK perspective because they are high value-added relative to other exports, such as textiles and labor, the United States would likely oppose these exports on the grounds that the proceeds could be more readily diverted to military use.

Similar concerns about diversion to military use led to a lower ranking for petroleum and science and technology imports. However, infrastructure aid of certain types, such as energy and transportation support clearly intended for civilian use, was broadly embraced as the action plan that would be supported by all sides.

Regarding the diplomacy and public diplomacy category, the experts generally agreed with prior RAND analysis that both action plans were useful. Their preference for liaison offices arose from the plan's greater short-term value in facilitating the implementation of agreements.

The public diplomacy action plans were also viewed by experts as generally useful. The preference for people-to-people exchanges arose from the consideration that this was easier to implement, as already experienced in the 2018 Winter Olympics, with strong popular impact.

Building Consensus Among In-Country Stakeholders

The second step was to test the resilience of these action plans to in-country stresses that could arise because of resistance from in-country stakeholders.

We asked experts to assess which action plans were likely to meet internal resistance and which were likely to have high levels of internal consensus. To this end, experts ranked the likely prioritization of the action plans among in-country stakeholders. Those action plans that were ranked differently by in-country stakeholders in comparison with the political leadership were likely to meet greater internal resistance to implementation, according to the experts. On the other hand, those action plans that in country-stakeholders ranked similarly in comparison with the political leadership would meet less internal resistance to implementation.

We used a statistical method, built around the coefficient of variation, to derive a consensus estimate behind an action plan. A higher percentage indicates higher in-country support. The experts arbitrarily chose a cut-off percentage of 75 percent consensus to screen action plans for inclusion in the next stage of portfolio construction. This meant that if the consensus was less than 75 percent within any country, the action plan was excluded from further consideration.

The consensus threshold helps ensure that the action plans are resilient to internal stresses. A problem in the past was that promised measures faced resistance from domestic stakeholders, leading to delays in implementation. For example, shipments of heavy fuel oil promised to North Korea under the Agreed Framework were delayed frequently because of congressional reluctance to fund such assistance.[36] Our approach explicitly seeks to avoid such problems.

Admittedly, this is a simplification of how negotiations will proceed in reality. However, it is useful for demonstrating the importance of considering the issue of in-country consensus, as well as for illustrating some useful areas in which consensus levels might be low.

The statistical method is described in Appendix C. The results are shown in Table 3.7.

Table 3.7 shows considerable variation in stakeholder consensus, both within and across countries. Not surprisingly, the two democratic countries (the ROK and United States) showed more variation, consistent with greater variations of views in those countries.

National defense action plans that reduce the DPRK's threat attain high levels of consensus in all countries. Those that reduce threats to the DPRK from the United States and ROK received lower levels of consensus in the United States and ROK, indicating the polarization within these countries. This led to the exclusion of one such action plan, the reduction of U.S. and ROK conventional capacity, from further consideration.

Regarding the diplomacy action plans, there was weaker consensus across the board, particularly arising from likely opposition from the military in all countries. In the case of the ROK, there was weak support from opposition parties as well. In consequence, both diplomacy action plans fell below the level of consensus needed for inclusion. The public diplomacy action plans both passed the consensus test, though with lower consensus levels in the United States and ROK. The economy actions plans mostly failed the consensus tests in the United States, indicating that the resilience of economy action plans

---

[36] See, for example, Robert Gallucci's comments in Frontline, undated.

Table 3.7
In-Country Support for Action Plans

	Consensus (%)			
Action Plan	**DPRK**	**United States**	**China**	**ROK**
Partially dismantle Yongbyon	84	92	100	91
DPRK reduces nuclear stockpile	90	94	98	96
DPRK reduces conventional capacity	95	98	98	92
Inspections of Punggye-ri	86	97	100	94
United States and ROK reduce major military exercises	95	82	100	75
United States and ROK reduce conventional capacity	100	69	100	81
United States and DPRK establish liaison offices	65	76	80	63
End-of-war declaration	74	68	80	61
People-to-people exchanges	100	75	100	75
Positive information campaigns	100	95	100	76
Exports: coal	94	50	94	81
Exports: metals	94	50	98	85
Exports: textiles	92	77	100	80
Exports: labor	94	77	100	81
Imports: petroleum	96	62	100	83
Imports: capital goods	93	73	83	77
Imports: science and technology	95	44	68	81
Imports: luxury goods	82	70	90	84
Financial flows	90	64	84	75
Infrastructure aid	96	91	90	82

NOTE: We used a statistical measure, the coefficient of variation, to derive consensus. The measure and its application are discussed in Appendix B. Those plans with less than 75 percent consensus in some country are shaded red. Consensus levels only measure the support for the views of the political leadership on an action plan. They do not measure support for the action plan or the scale of outcomes.

could be low there. In particular, the major export and import items (coal, metals, and petroleum) failed to pass the consensus test.

After applying the consensus tests, the surviving action plans are shown in Table 3.8.

The next step, the recommendation of portfolios by experts, involved a consideration of trade-offs within and across the diplomatic, economic, and national security components.

The recommended portfolios are presented in Box 3.2. As noted earlier and emphasized by the expert panel, negotiations at the official level would involve a level of detail that was missing in these recommendations. Therefore, these recommendations are best viewed as directional and are intended to show how the methodology can lead to recommended portfolios.

All three portfolios contain diplomatic, economic, and security action plans. The first portfolio offers a greater number of trade-offs than Portfolios 2 and 3 but also requires more ongoing commitments, such as a long-term reduction in military exercises and monitoring the state of the Yongbyon facility. The second portfolio offers fewer trade-offs in return for fewer ongoing commitments and quicker implementation. The third portfolio splits the difference. It balances a big achievement for the U.S.-ROK alliance with a big achievement for the DPRK and has one ongoing commitment.

Table 3.8
Expert-Ranked Action Plans After Consensus Tests

Rank	National Defense	Economy	Public Diplomacy
1	Partially dismantle Yongbyon	Provide infrastructure aid	People-to-people exchanges
2	DPRK reduces nuclear stockpile	Textile exports	Positive information campaigns
3	United States and ROK reduce major military exercises	Labor exports	
4	Inspections of Punggye-ri		
5	DPRK reduces conventional capacity		

Box 3.2
Proposed Portfolios

Portfolio 1

- Partially dismantle Yongbyon.
- United States and ROK reduce major military exercises.
- Provide infrastructure aid.
- Allow textile exports.
- Foster people-to-people exchanges.
- Create positive information campaigns.

Portfolio 2

- Reduce nuclear stockpile.
- Inspect Punggye-ri.
- Allow labor exports.
- Create positive information campaigns.

Portfolio 3

- Partially dismantle Yongbyon.
- Provide infrastructure aid.
- Foster people-to-people exchanges.

Each portfolio contains at least one win-win action plan. These are the public diplomacy action plans. Partially dismantling Yongbyon is a big loss for the DPRK. In exchange for this loss in Portfolio 1, the DPRK obtains economic support (infrastructure aid) and sanctions relief (textile exports), as well as security gains (continued reduction of U.S.-ROK military exercises). In Portfolio 3, the DPRK obtains only infrastructure aid in return. This likely means that the level of dismantlement of Yongbyon would be relatively lower than in Portfolio 1 and/or the level of infrastructure aid would have to be much more significant than the infrastructure aid envisaged in Portfolio 1.

Portfolio 2 requires the DPRK to make two smaller concessions (a reduced nuclear stockpile and inspection of Punggye-ri) in return for sanctions relief on labor exports.

Although the implementation strategies are outside the scope of this report, the expert panel recommended some important roles that stakeholder countries could play with regard to ensuring that the agreements succeed. These roles are shown in Table 3.9.

Table 3.9 suggests a substantial role for each of the four stakeholder countries. Although the roles of the United States and DPRK are obvious, some panelists argued that the failure of the 2018–2019 dialogues was because of the peripheral roles played by China and the ROK. It was noted that China is the only country that North Korea would trust to play the role of guarantor of its sovereignty through the process of denuclearization. China and the ROK would also play key roles in the economic development of North Korea.

Table 3.9
Roles of Stakeholder Countries

	Monitoring and Compliance	Participation in Action Plans	Guarantor
China	DPRK and U.S.-ROK adherence	National defense, economic	DPRK sovereignty
DPRK	U.S.-ROK adherence	National defense, economic, public diplomacy	
ROK	DPRK adherence	National defense, economic, public diplomacy	
United States	DPRK adherence	National defense, public diplomacy	ROK sovereignty
International bodies	DPRK and U.S.-ROK adherence		

CHAPTER FOUR

Conclusion

Twenty-six years have passed since the United States and North Korea signed their first agreement, the Agreed Framework, intended to denuclearize North Korea in return for economic assistance. That agreement collapsed, though not without interim gains. As of 2020, despite several official dialogues, no agreement is in place, and the two countries again face rising tension.

In this report, we explored the opportunities for conflict resolution and consensus-building between North Korea and the United States. The purpose of this study is methodological: to explore whether a different framework of negotiations would make a difference. We proposed and tested an approach to negotiations that was designed to address the reasons for past failures and that reflects current realities. We term this approach the *portfolio method.*

In our assessment of past failures, we identified three principal reasons for failure that would need to be addressed in future negotiations: (1) disagreements on the goals of negotiations, (2) inadequate domestic and international support (both state and nonstate), and (3) the failure to use trust-building mechanisms. Using this analysis of past failures, we developed several key elements that should be part of the framework for any new negotiations. The portfolio method's elements are (1) the inclusion of countries with national interests that overlap those of the United States and North Korea, (2) prior agreement on the goals of negotiation between the negotiating parties, (3) the inclusion of primarily hard commitments in agreements, (4) the incorporation of the preferences of in-country stakeholders, (5) the linking of multiple areas of negotiation, and (6) trust-building mechanisms.

To test the portfolio method, we assembled a team of experts, who went through the steps for portfolio creation with actual cases using the portfolio method and provided a review. We used the method of Track II dialogue.

To develop and test the portfolio method, we prepared a logic model (Chapter Two), then undertook the following tasks (Chapter Three):

1. identified countries and in-country stakeholders
2. developed the negotiation goals
3. listed and assessed action plans
4. developed and recommended action plans and portfolios.

Steps 1–3 were based on research and validated by a team of experts. For Step 4, the team of experts jointly reviewed the action plans and developed portfolios. The actions plans were subjected to a consensus test and then ranked by expert preferences within portfolios.

This exercise resulted in the recommendation of three portfolios. Each contains diplomatic, economic, and security components. The expert panel also recommended roles that each stakeholder country would play in the implementation of the agreement.

The expert dialogue was generally supportive of the portfolio method and its key elements because it made explicit the condition that official negotiations on action plans must be based on a pre-agreed framework of goals and other elements. The experts also welcomed the insights that considering trade-offs brought to the analysis, such as recognizing a country's bargaining power.

In summary, we propose in this report an approach that explicitly addresses the reasons for past failures. The portfolio method does so by developing portfolios of action plans that reflect stakeholder goals and priorities and that include the diplomatic, economic, and security domains. The portfolios are constructed with the help of expert dialogue. We find that the portfolio method offers promising ways forward in negotiations with North Korea.

APPENDIX A

Screening of Action Plans

The initial screening of action plans is based on the CRIVR criteria, as follows: (1) contributes to the goals, individually and jointly, (2) reciprocity of gains and losses from the portfolio of action plans, (3) implementable in one year or less at low cost, (4) verifiability, and (5) reversibility or low-cost replaceability.

Table A.1 shows the result of the screening exercise, which we undertook for four of the five criteria (excluding reciprocity, which is applicable at the portfolio level). Action plans that are shaded yellow did not meet the test.

Table A.1
CRIVR Screening of Action Plans

Action Plan	Category	Contributes to Goals	Implementable	Verifiable	Reversible
The DPRK partially dismantles Yongbyon nuclear facilities under international inspection.	National defense	Y	Y	Y	Y
The DPRK destroys a certain number of warheads.	National defense	Y	Y	Y	Y
The DPRK allows inspection on the newly identified nuclear facilities (for example, the ones brought up by the United States during Hanoi Summit).	National defense	Y	Y	N	Y
The DPRK allows international inspection of the Punggye-ri nuclear test site.	National defense	Y	Y	Y	Y
The United States and ROK reduce major military exercises.	National defense	Y	Y	Y	Y
The United States and ROK reduce military capability in the peninsula.	National defense	Y	Y	Y	Y
The DPRK stops producing nuclear materials and developing missile capabilities.	National defense	Y	Y	N	Y
The DPRK provides the full list of its nuclear facilities.	National defense	Y	Y	N	N
The DPRK reduces conventional weapons capability.	National defense	Y	Y	N	Y

Table A.1—Continued

Action Plan	Category	Contributes to Goals	Implementable	Verifiable	Reversible
The DPRK reduces military exercises.	National defense	Y	Y	Y	Y
The United States and DPRK establish liaison offices.	Diplomacy	Y	Y	Y	Y
An end-of-war declaration.	Diplomacy	Y	Y	Y	Y
The United States and DPRK sign a peace treaty.	Diplomacy	Y	Y	Y	N
Economic sanctions relief for the DPRK, for a limited time.	Economy	Y	Y	Y	Y
Provide infrastructure aid to the DPRK.	Economy	Y	Y	Y	Y
Initiate a program of people-to-people exchanges.	Public diplomacy	Y	Y	Y	Y
Initiate positive information campaigns.	Public diplomacy	Y	Y	Y	Y

APPENDIX B

Measuring Consensus Among In-Country Stakeholders

The support of in-country stakeholders for the actions of the country's political leadership is important for determining whether the decisions of the political leadership will be followed through by (1) those responsible for implementing decisions and (2) those whose support is needed to sustain support for agreements. In this report, we identified stakeholders for each negotiating country and argued that a minimum level of consensus among in-country stakeholders is necessary if action plans are to be resilient to changes within a country, such as a change in political leadership.

To ascertain resilience, we asked experts to rank each action plan on a Likert scale, as follows:

1. strongly against, lowest priority, or least preferred
2. moderately or somewhat against
3. neutral
4. moderately for or somewhat preferred
5. strongly for, highest priority, or most preferred.

Ranks capture relative priorities among action plans. They are *not* measures of the likelihood or size of an outcome.

The experts ranked each of the in-country stakeholders. We then used the rankings to calculate the consensus of in-country stakeholders behind the country's political leadership, using the following formula:

Consensus (percentage) = (1 – (*sd* / *rankpl*)) × 100, where *sd* = standard deviation of ranks of the population and *rankpl* = rank of the political leadership.

This approach is not the only way to measure consensus. The academic literature offers a variety of ways to calculate the level of consensus (or its complement, the level of disagreement) of Likert-ranked preferences, many of which are built around the standard deviation and covariance.[1] These methods include the F-test for equality of standard deviations, the intraclass correlation coefficient, and the coefficient of variation for deviation of a variable from some underlying mean value.

We used a threshold of 75 percent consensus in each country for inclusion of an action plan in the list for negotiation.[2]

The consensus levels for each action plan are shown in Table 3.7.

---

[1] See Hiral A. Shah and Sema A. Kalaian, "Which Is the Best Parametric Statistical Method for Analyzing Delphi Data?" *Journal of Modern Applied Statistical Methods*, Vol. 8, No. 1, May 2009; and Mushtaq Abdal Rahem and Marjorie Darrah, "Using a Computational Approach for Generalizing a Consensus Measure to Likert Scales of Any Size *n*," *International Journal of Mathematics and Mathematical Sciences*, Vol. 2018, 2018.

The use of the standard deviation as a measure of disagreement is most suitable when the measurement error does not vary by the respondent. See Teresa Henriques, Luis Antunes, João Bernardes, Mara Matias, Diogo Sato, and Cristina Costa-Santos, "Information-Based Measure of Disagreement for More Than Two Observers: A Useful Tool to Compare the Degree of Observer Disagreement," *BMC Medical Research Methodology*, Vol. 13, Article 47, 2013.

[2] Disagreement rates below 25 percent are viewed as sufficient for comparative use. See Matthew Graham, Anthony Milanowski, and Jackson Miller, *Measuring and Promoting Inter-Rater Agreement of Teacher and Principal Performance Ratings*, Center for Educator Compensation Reform, February 2012.

APPENDIX C

Glossary

Action plan	See *short-term action plan.*
Categories of action plans	Action plans belong to one of four categories: national defense, diplomacy, economy, or public diplomacy.
CRIVR	CRIVR is an acronym for the constraints on action plans and portfolios. The criteria are fulfilled if the portfolio fulfills the following conditions: (1) **C**ontributes to the negotiation goals, individually and jointly, (2) **R**eciprocity of gains and losses from the portfolio of action plans, (3) **I**mplementable in the short-term at low cost, (4) **V**erifiability, and (5) **R**eversibility or low-cost replaceability.
Feasible portfolio	A portfolio that meets feasibility criteria
In-country stakeholder	Groups with influence on policymaking within a stakeholder country

Level of consensus within a country	1 minus the coefficient of variation around the ranking of the political leadership, expressed as a percentage: Consensus = (1 – (*sd*/*rankpl*)) × 100, where *sd* = standard deviation of ranks of the population and *rankpl* = rank of the political leadership.
Long-term goal	Desired outcome over a period that is not immediately foreseeable
Negotiation goal	See *short-term goal*.
Portfolio	A combination of two or more short-term action plans
Priorities	Highly ranked goals (short or long term)
Short-term action plan	Also simply referred to as an *action plan*, this is a course of action (with associated timelines and resources needed) that can be implemented within 12 months and that addresses the short-term goals (or negotiation goals).
Short-term goal	Desired outcomes that can be fulfilled within a foreseeable period
Stakeholder country	Countries that have been identified as engagement partners in the negotiations

References

Abdal Rahem, Mushtaq, and Marjorie Darrah, "Using a Computational Approach for Generalizing a Consensus Measure to Likert Scales of Any Size *n*," *International Journal of Mathematics and Mathematical Sciences*, Vol. 2018, 2018.

Arms Control Association, "The U.S.-North Korean Agreed Framework at a Glance," fact sheet, last reviewed July 2018. As of September 23, 2020: https://www.armscontrol.org/factsheets/agreedframework

Bae, Kook-Yeol, "A Study of the Economic Elites in the Kim Jong-il Era [in Korean]," *Association of North Korean Studies*, Vol. 35, No. 2, December 30, 2010, pp. 75–101.

Bartolini, Stefano, *Restructuring Europe: Centre Formation, System Building, and Political Structuring Between the Nation State and the European Union*, Oxford, United Kingdom: Oxford University Press, 2005.

Blakemore, Erin, "Bill Clinton Once Struck a Nuclear Deal with North Korea," History.com, updated September 1, 2018. As of September 10, 2020: https://www.history.com/news/north-korea-nuclear-deal-bill-clinton-agreed-framework

Blomquist, Rachel, and Daniel Wertz, "An Overview of North Korea-Japan Relations," National Committee on North Korea, updated June 2015. As of September 10, 2020: https://www.ncnk.org/resources/briefing-papers/all-briefing-papers/overview-north-korea-japan-relations

Carlin, Robert, and John W. Lewis, *Negotiating with North Korea: 1992–2007*, Stanford, Calif.: Center for International Security and Cooperation, Stanford University, January 2008.

Chan, Tara Francis, "What Goes on Inside the Secretive, Semi-Official Talks Between the North Korea, the US, and South Korea," *Business Insider*, March 19, 2018. As of September 10, 2020: https://www.businessinsider.sg/what-does-track-2-talks-mean-north-korea-2018-3

Chandran, Nyshka, "Seoul Is Relying on Big Companies to Invest in North Korea, so Promised Reforms Are Taking a Backseat," *CNBC*, October 9, 2018. As of September 10, 2020:
https://www.cnbc.com/2018/10/10/seoul-relies-on-chaebols-for-north-korea-investment-so-reform-doubtful.html

Elmer, Keegan, "Chinese President Xi Jinping Gives North Korean Leader Kim Jong-Un His Full Support," *South China Morning Post*, June 19, 2019. As of September 10, 2020:
https://www.scmp.com/news/china/diplomacy/article/3015159/chinese-president-xi-jinping-gives-north-korean-leader-kim

Financial Action Task Force, *International Standards on Combating Money Laundering and the Financing of Terrorism & Proliferation*, Paris, updated June 2019. As of September 10, 2020:
http://www.fatf-gafi.org/publications/fatfrecommendations/documents/fatf-recommendations.html

Friedman, Uri, "What Does 'Denuclearization' Mean to Kim Jong Un?" *The Atlantic*, March 28, 2018. As of September 10, 2020:
https://www.theatlantic.com/international/archive/2018/03/kim-jong-un-china-xi-jinping-train-nuclear-trump-summit/556679/

Frontline, "Examining the Lessons of the 1994 U.S.-North Korea Deal," webpage, undated. As of September 10, 2020:
https://www.pbs.org/wgbh/pages/frontline/shows/kim/themes/lessons.html

Gallucci, Robert L., "Lessons to Be Learned from Negotiating with North Korea," *38 North*, September 17, 2019. As of September 10, 2020:
https://www.38north.org/2019/09/rgallucci091719/

Graham, Matthew, Anthony Milanowski, and Jackson Miller, *Measuring and Promoting Inter-Rater Agreement of Teacher and Principal Performance Ratings*, Center for Educator Compensation Reform, February 2012.

Henriques, Teresa, Luis Antunes, João Bernardes, Mara Matias, Diogo Sato, and Cristina Costa-Santos, "Information-Based Measure of Disagreement for More Than Two Observers: A Useful Tool to Compare the Degree of Observer Disagreement," *BMC Medical Research Methodology*, Vol. 13, Article 47, 2013.

Homans, Charles, "Track II Diplomacy: A Short History," *Foreign Policy*, June 20, 2011. As of September 10, 2020:
https://foreignpolicy.com/2011/06/20/track-ii-diplomacy-a-short-history/

Human Rights First, "North Korean Workers Earn Millions for Their Government Overseas," October 31, 2017. As of September 10, 2020:
https://www.humanrightsfirst.org/blog/north-korean-workers-earn-millions-their-government-overseas

International Crisis Group, *North Korea: Beyond the Six Party Talks*, Brussels, June 16, 2015. As of September 10, 2020: https://www.crisisgroup.org/asia/north-east-asia/korean-peninsula/north-korea-beyond-six-party-talks

Jeong, Hyung-Gon, Byung-Yeon Kim, and Suk Lee, *The Current Situation of Marketization in North Korea and Prospects for Change of Its Economic System*, Seoul: Korea Institute for International Economic Policy, World Economy Update 13-10, 2013.

Ji, Dagyum, "Seoul 'Must Stop' Joint U.S.-ROK Military Drills: DPRK Media," *NK News*, January 11, 2018. As of September 10, 2020: https://www.nknews.org/2018/01/seoul-must-stop-joint-u-s-rok-military-drills-dprk-media/

Kekic, Laza, "The Economist Intelligence Unit's Index of Democracy," *The Economist*, 2007. As of September 24, 2020: https://www.economist.com/media/pdf/DEMOCRACY_INDEX_2007_v3.pdf

King, Robert R., "North Koreans Want External Information, but Kim Jong-Un Seeks to Limit Access," Center for Strategic and International Studies, May 15, 2019. As of September 10, 2020: https://www.csis.org/analysis/north-koreans-want-external-information-kim-jong-un-seeks-limit-access

Klingner, Bruce, "Why Does North Korea Want Nukes?" Heritage Foundation, August 13, 2018. As of September 10, 2020: https://www.heritage.org/insider/summer-2018-insider/why-does-north-korea-want-nukes

Korean Statistical Information Service, homepage, undated. As of September 29, 2020: https://kosis.kr/eng/

Kudláčová, Lenka, "South Korean Civil Society Organizations as Confidence-Builders? The Experience with South Korean Civil Society Groupings in the Republic of Korea and the DPRK," *Perspectives*, Vol. 22, No. 2, 2014, pp. 33–64.

Kuhn, Anthony, "In 'Terrific Explosion,' North Korea Blows Up Liaison Office," *National Public Radio*, June 16, 2020. As of September 24, 2020: https://www.npr.org/2020/06/16/877887300/in-terrific-explosion-north-korea-blows-up-liaison-office

Lam, Katherine, "Kim Jong Un Killed Uncle, Half-Brother over 'China Coup Plot,' Report Says," *Fox News*, updated September 25, 2017. As of September 10, 2020: https://www.foxnews.com/world/kim-jong-un-killed-uncle-half-brother-over-china-coup-plot-report-says

McEachern, Patrick, "North Korea's Policy Process: Assessing Institutional Policy Preferences," *Asian Survey*, Vol. 49, No. 3, May/June 2009, pp. 528–552.

Miller, J. Berkshire, "Japan's North Korean Anxieties," *American Interest*, May 15, 2018. As of September 10, 2020:
https://www.the-american-interest.com/2018/05/15/japans-north-korean-anxieties/

Montville, Joseph V., "Track Two Diplomacy: The Work of Healing History," *Journal of Diplomacy and International Relations*, Vol. 7, No. 2, Summer/Fall 2006, pp. 15–25.

Mount, Adam, *Conventional Deterrence of North Korea*, Washington, D.C.: Federation of American Scientists, 2019. As of September 10, 2020:
https://fas.org/wp-content/uploads/2019/12/FAS-CDNK.pdf

Nikitin, Mary Beth D., Emma Chanlett-Avery, and Mark E. Manyin, *Nuclear Negotiations with North Korea: In Brief*, Washington, D.C.: Congressional Research Service, December 4, 2017.

"North Korea Nuclear Test Tunnels at Punggye-ri 'Destroyed,'" *BBC*, May 24, 2018. As of September 10, 2020:
https://www.bbc.com/news/world-asia-44240047

Observatory of Economic Complexity, "Where Does North Korea Export To?" webpage, undated. As of September 10, 2020:
https://oec.world/en/visualize/tree_map/hs92/export/prk/show/all/2000/

O'Carroll, Chad, "Military Drills Will Lead to 'Unimaginable Holocaust,' Says N. Korea," *NK News*, January 16, 2014. As of September 10, 2020:
https://www.nknews.org/2014/01/
military-drills-will-lead-to-unimaginable-holocaust-says-n-korea/

Osaki, Tomohiro, "Japan, China and South Korea Are 'in Sync' on North Korea, Japanese Official Says," *Japan Times*, May 9, 2018. As of September 10, 2020:
https://www.japantimes.co.jp/news/2018/05/09/national/politics-diplomacy/japan-hosts-leaders-china-south-korea-summit-north-korea/#.XaNijS3MyF0

Parkhe, Arvind, "Building Trust in International Alliances," *Journal of World Business*, Vol. 33, No. 4, Winter 1998, pp. 417–437.

Sang-Hun, Choe, "North Korea's State-Run Economy Falters Under Sanctions, Testing Elite Loyalty," *New York Times*, April 18, 2019. As of September 10, 2020:
https://www.nytimes.com/2019/04/18/world/asia/north-korea-economy-sanctions.html

Scobell, Andrew, "China and North Korea: Bolstering a Buffer or Hunkering Down in Northeast Asia?" testimony presented before the U.S.-China Economic and Security Review Commission on June 8, 2017, Santa Monica, Calif.: RAND Corporation, CT-477, 2017. As of September 10, 2020:
https://www.rand.org/pubs/testimonies/CT477.html

Shah, Hiral A., and Sema A. Kalaian, "Which Is the Best Parametric Statistical Method for Analyzing Delphi Data?" *Journal of Modern Applied Statistical Methods*, Vol. 8, No. 1, May 2009, pp. 226–232.

Shifrinson, Joshua, "Security in Northeast Asia: Structuring a Settlement," *Strategic Studies Quarterly*, Vol. 13, No. 2, Summer 2019, pp. 23–47.

Snyder, Scott A., "The Motivations Behind North Korea's Pursuit of Simultaneous Economic and Nuclear Development," *Asia Unbound*, Council on Foreign Relations blog, November 20, 2013. As of September 24, 2020: https://www.cfr.org/blog/motivations-behind-north-koreas-pursuit-simultaneous-economic-and-nuclear-development

———, "Human Rights Conditions of Overseas Laborers from North Korea," *Asia Unbound*, Council on Foreign Relations blog, May 22, 2015. As of September 10, 2020:
https://www.cfr.org/blog/human-rights-conditions-overseas-laborers-north-korea

Steger, Isabella, "North and South Korea Agreed to Work on Formally Ending the Korean War," *Quartz*, April 27, 2018. As of September 10, 2020: https://qz.com/1264087/korea-summit-full-text-of-kim-jong-un-and-moon-jae-ins-joint-statement-the-panmunjom-declaration/

Turk, Lynn, "North Korea: Liaison Offices—the First Time," *38 North*, June 29, 2018. As of September 10, 2020:
https://www.38north.org/2018/06/lturk062918/

United Nations, "UN Comtrade Database," webpage, undated. As of September 29, 2020:
https://comtrade.un.org

United Nations Security Council, Resolution 2094 (2013), March 7, 2013. As of September 10, 2020:
https://undocs.org/S/RES/2094(2013)

———, Resolution 2270 (2016), March 2, 2016a. As of September 10, 2020: https://undocs.org/S/RES/2270(2016)

———, Resolution 2321 (2016), November 30, 2016b. As of September 10, 2020: https://www.undocs.org/S/RES/2321(2016)

———, Resolution 2371 (2017), August 5, 2017a. As of September 10, 2020: https://undocs.org/S/RES/2371(2017)

———, Resolution 2375 (2017), September 11, 2017b. As of September 10, 2020: https://www.undocs.org/S/RES/2375%20(2017)

———, Resolution 2397 (2017), December 22, 2017c. As of September 10, 2020: https://undocs.org/S/RES/2397(2017)

UNSC—*See* United Nations Security Council.

U.S. Department of State, Bureau of Arms Control, Verification, and Compliance, "Agreed Framework Between the United States of America and the Democratic People's Republic of Korea," Washington, D.C., October 21, 1994. As of September 10, 2020:
https://2001-2009.state.gov/t/ac/rls/or/2004/31009.htm

U.S. Department of State, Office of the Spokesman, "Initial Actions to Implement Six-Party Joint Statement," Washington, D.C., February 13, 2007. As of September 10, 2020:
https://2001-2009.state.gov/r/pa/prs/ps/2007/february/80508.htm

U.S. Office of the Director of National Intelligence, *Worldwide Threat Assessment of the U.S. Intelligence Community*, Washington, D.C., January 29, 2019. As of September 10, 2020:
https://www.dni.gov/files/ODNI/documents/2019-ATA-SFR---SSCI.pdf

Whitehead, Laurence, "Democratization and Human Rights in the Americas: Should the Jury Still Be Out?" in Louise Fawcett and Mónica Serrano, eds., *Regionalism and Governance in the Americas: Continental Drift*, London: Palgrave Macmillan, 2005, pp. 161–184.

White House, "Joint Statement of President Donald J. Trump of the United States of America and Chairman Kim Jong Un of the Democratic People's Republic of Korea at the Singapore Summit," Singapore, June 12, 2018. As of September 10, 2020:
https://www.whitehouse.gov/briefings-statements/joint-statement-president-donald-j-trump-united-states-america-chairman-kim-jong-un-democratic-peoples-republic-korea-singapore-summit/

Wakin, Daniel J., and Sheryl Gay Stolberg, "North Koreans Welcome Symphonic Diplomacy," *New York Times*, February 27, 2008. As of September 10, 2020:
https://www.nytimes.com/2008/02/27/world/asia/27symphony.html

Wee, Heesun, "How Kim Jong Un Wants to Develop His Economy and Secure His Regime," *CNBC*, June 11, 2018. As of September 10, 2020:
https://www.cnbc.com/2018/06/11/how-kim-jong-un-wants-to-develop-his-economy-and-secure-his-regime.html

Zwirko, Colin, "286 Meetings Held at Inter-Korean Liaison Office Since September: MOU," *NK News*, December 20, 2018. As of September 10, 2020:
https://www.nknews.org/2018/12/285-meetings-held-at-inter-korean-liaison-office-since-september-mou/?c=1568151244139